THE

GARDENS

OF

COLONIAL

WILLIAMSBURG

THE
GARDENS
of
COLONIAL
WILLIAMSBURG

BY M. KENT BRINKLEY

AND GORDON W. CHAPPELL

Photography by David M. Doody

Additional photography
by Tom Green and the staff of the
Colonial Williamsburg Foundation

THE COLONIAL WILLIAMSBURG FOUNDATION

WILLIAMSBURG, VIRGINIA

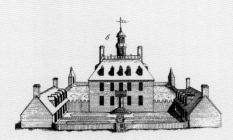

THIS BOOK ABOUT THESE WIDELY KNOWN
AND APPRECIATED GARDENS IS DEDICATED TO THE SEVERAL
GENERATIONS, PAST AND PRESENT, OF LANDSCAPE ARCHITECTS, HOR-
TICULTURISTS, AND GARDENERS WHO HAVE LEFT THEIR MARK UPON
THE LANDSCAPE HERE AT COLONIAL WILLIAMSBURG. WITHOUT THE
VISION, CREATIVITY, AND STEWARDSHIP OF THIS TALENTED AND
DEDICATED GROUP OF PROFESSIONALS, COLONIAL WILLIAMSBURG'S
RECONSTRUCTED GARDENS AND LANDSCAPES—AND THIS BOOK
ABOUT THEM—WOULD NOT EXIST.

The Gardens of Colonial Williamsburg
© 1996 by The Colonial Williamsburg Foundation
Fourth Printing, 2003

Library of Congress Cataloging-in-Publication Data

Brinkley, M. Kent
    The Gardens of Colonial Williamsburg / by M. Kent Brinkley
and Gordon W. Chappell ; photography by David M. Doody ; additional photography by
Tom Green and the staff of the Colonial Williamsburg Foundation.
            p.   cm.
    Includes bibliographical references and index
    ISBN 0-87935-158-6 (hc)
    1. Gardens—Virginia—Williamsburg.   I. Chappell, Gordon W.
II. Colonial Williamsburg Foundation. III. Title.
SB466.U65W2 1996
712' .6' 0975554252--dc20   95-34111
                                                              CIP

Book design by K.C. Witherell

Printed in China

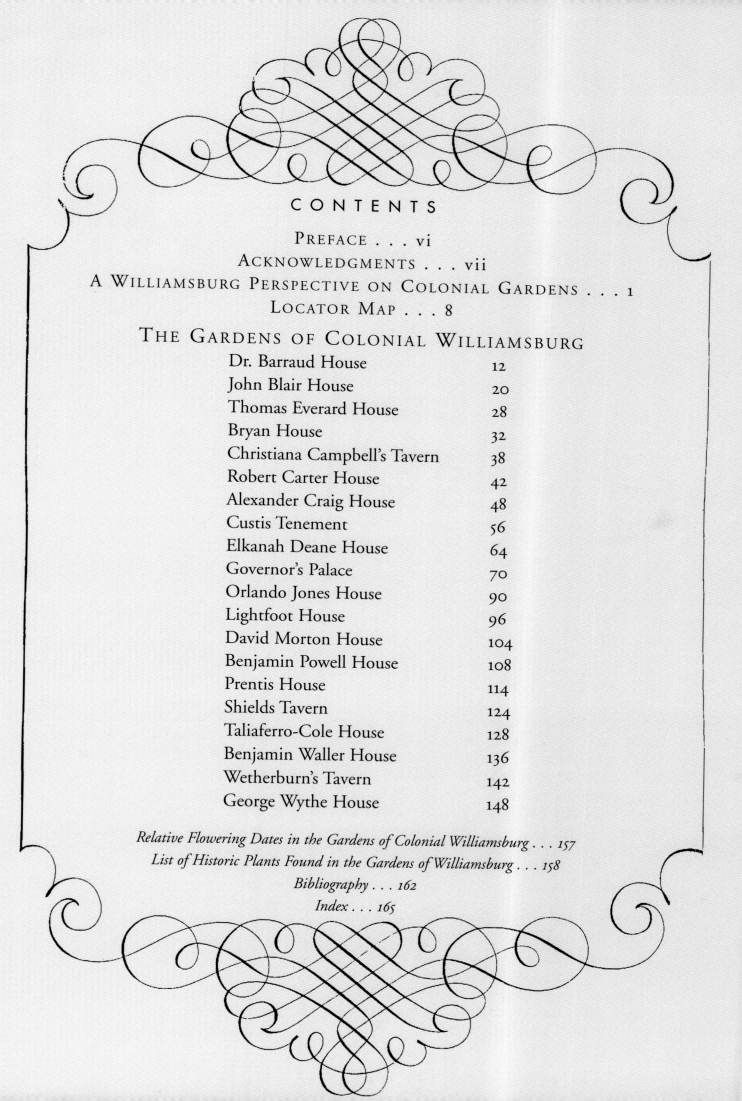

CONTENTS

Gardeners and everyone who delights in the enchantment of plants and flowers will find much to interest them in the gardens of Colonial Williamsburg. In eighteenth-century Virginia, gardening was appreciated and practiced in many diverse ways. Among the gentry, gardening was seen as an art, and their gardens were constructed to precise rules of design. Formality characterized their layouts and plantings. Among the common folk in Williamsburg, gardens may have reflected some ornamental aspects, but they were largely devoted to growing vegetables and fruits. Regardless of the degree of design refinements, these gardens had a common theme: they were tangible expressions of the colonists' ability to control the wilderness that still surrounded them. Though the gardens of the Virginia colonists followed the design principles then in vogue in England, in the end the Virginia garden acquired a unique look all its own.

Because of its very reliance on living plants to provide its framework, gardening is an ephemeral art. Plants eventually die, and gardens vanish all too quickly unless given constant care and attention. Rare is the garden which long outlives its creator. Rarer still is a garden which survives in its original form for a hundred years or more. When the restoration of Williamsburg began, the eighteenth-century landscape had vanished. Lacking surviving garden features, the landscape architects began intense research to learn about eighteenth-century gardens. As important as they knew their work to be, they probably never realized that they were establishing the new field of historic landscape restoration in America. The efforts of those pioneers are recorded in Colonial Williamsburg's re-created gardens. These gardens, some now sixty-five years old, have been the source of constant change, and have the maintenance requirements peculiar to mature landscapes. They survive and flourish through the dedicated efforts of a staff of professional gardeners who maintain them.

The designers of these gardens sought to re-create Williamsburg's eighteenth-century landscapes, yet they also gave rise to a unique design style, known today as "colonial revival." Aside from the design ideas and the glimpses of the past they provide, the gardens of Colonial Williamsburg are compelling examples of a unique landscape architectural style, and present details of our colonial past as they were interpreted in the formative stages of the American preservation movement. These gardens can be appreciated in many varied ways: to pass along horticultural and landscape design knowledge, to provide insights into the everyday life of another age, and to help us understand the visions and philosophies that gave rise to preserving our historic past.

This book will introduce you to Colonial Williamsburg's re-created gardens. Twenty of Colonial Williamsburg's best-known gardens—listed in alphabetical order—are included in the book. Most are colonial revival re-creations based on colonial and English precedents, and some are gardens more recently developed based primarily on documentary evidence. The opening chapter endeavors to set the context for the gardens with a bit of organizational history and garden history. Each garden section includes notes about the eighteenth-century citizens who lived and gardened on that property. Documentary research details and archaeological findings are presented in hopes that their importance will become self-evident. A description of the gardens accompanies a plan keyed to a list of the buildings, garden spaces, and major plants. The appendix includes a comprehensive list of the plants found in the gardens, a relative bloom schedule for the gardens, and a detailed bibliography, should this book stimulate further interest in the subject.

Enjoyable, rewarding discoveries await you in Colonial Williamsburg's gardens. We hope the book will guide you as you return to experience the sights, smells, colors, and textures found in the gardens each season of the year.

ACKNOWLEDGMENTS

Although we lived with this book project from start to finish, few books are written without the help and support of many others. Throughout the five-year period that we worked to prepare this book for publication, we gratefully received help from many colleagues we are pleased to acknowledge.

We especially extend our sincere thanks and appreciation to Dave Doody and Tom Green of the Audiovisual Programs Department for their time and talents that produced over six full seasons of garden photography for this book. The considerable efforts they devoted to this project captured the colors, moods, and essences of Colonial Williamsburg's gardens and contributed significantly to making the resulting book truly a visual delight.

A continuing source of encouragement came from William L. Roberts, Jr., Colonial Williamsburg's vice president for Administration and Finance. His admiration of these gardens and abiding interest in this book are the primary reasons this undertaking became more than just an idea in our minds.

Our editorial assistant for this project was Larry Griffith, senior gardener. Larry's help ranged from garden inspections and plant identification to repeatedly proofreading the manuscript and verifying botanical nomenclature. Carolin Shoosmith, our secretary, proofread the manuscript drafts several times to check our grammar and spelling.

Their efforts were an immense help.

Several key people worked patiently to focus our writing efforts and to refine the manuscript. Many of them critically read (and often reread) various drafts. A select few lent considerable research and editorial support in editing the final versions of the manuscript. Most notably, we offer our sincere thanks to Patricia

Gibbs, Cathleene Hellier, Emma Lou Powers, and Linda Rowe of the Department of Historical Research for their assistance.

In addition, thanks are due to the following in-house readers for their thoughtful comments and critiques—Marley R. Brown III, Gary Brumfield, Edward A. Chappell, and Lawrence Henry.

We also gratefully appreciate the guidance, substantial ideas, and conceptual contributions made by the Colonial Williamsburg Foundation's Publications Department staff. Several key staff members influenced the concept and the

scope of this book, and we would like to thank Donna Sheppard for tireless and thorough proofreading and copyediting and Joseph N. Rountree, director, for the many general suggestions made throughout the process. K.C. Witherell, designer, brought the project to life with her elegant book design.

It is also appropriate here to acknowledge the support for this book over the years by the current and former members of Colonial Williamsburg's Publications Committee under the chairmanship of D. Stephen Elliott, vice president, Education Division.

In addition, we would also like to express appreciation and thanks for the support that was given this project by former vice president William S. Gardiner and former director Willard E. Gwilliam, FAIA, both of whom have retired from the Colonial Williamsburg Foundation.

Finally, we are especially grateful for the support from several of our colleagues in the Landscape Services Department, including Robert Scott, director, Wesley Green and Rollin Woolley, landscape supervisors, Laura Viancour, coordinator of garden programs, Terry Yemm, landscape foreman, Thomas Brooks and Don McKelvey, senior gardeners, Scott Mowrey and Tony Craig, tree surgeons, and Libbey Oliver, manager of floral services. We are extremely grateful to all of these individuals for their logistical help and suggestions.

A WILLIAMSBURG PERSPECTIVE ON COLONIAL GARDENS

Gardens have always been an important aspect of the Williamsburg scene, both in the eighteenth century and today when at least three generations have come to appreciate this town and its gardens as an integral part of America's historical heritage. Colonial Williamsburg's political and historical legacy is well known, but despite its popularity, relatively few realize that in addition to being an important political and cultural center in eighteenth-century Virginia, Williamsburg was a center of gardening activity.

In the eighteenth century, Williamsburg was the capital of the largest, wealthiest, and most populous of the colonies and the center of cultural life in Virginia. But compared to Philadelphia or Charleston, Williamsburg remained a small, but beautiful, green country town. During the Revolution, the Virginia capital was moved to Richmond because it was felt that Williamsburg was too vulnerable to attacks from the British. With this move Williamsburg slowly changed into a quiet town that time and development seemed to forget. While few of the public buildings survived, many of the old homes and shops remained in use into the twentieth century.

Due to its prudent town plan, Williamsburg did not grow with the same hodgepodge disorder of the earlier Jamestown settlement. Lieutenant Governor Francis Nicholson's plan for Williamsburg was laid out around an orderly grouping of public buildings, each relating to the others in a spacious overall scheme. Characterized by its broad, straight streets and its impressive public buildings, the new capital had distinctly urban qualities. Its baroque-style vistas pulled the public buildings into the landscape, and the useful open spaces reflected current European city planning trends. Nicholson's early eighteenth-century plan is still largely intact, and Williamsburg today demonstrates how well conceived his planning vision truly was.

It is a credit to the conservative English taste of Williamsburg's gardeners that this small Virginia town had some of the best examples of Anglo-Dutch gardens in the colonies. This garden style, characterized by geometric symmetry within an enclosed space, was common in England in the late seventeenth and early eighteenth century. Historical evidence suggests that the emerging trend toward naturalistic gardens in contemporary England did not appeal to the settlers in Virginia. To those Virginians, a natural landscape did not need to be re-created; there were ample reminders of that at every turn. To them, a garden was nature tamed, trimmed, and enclosed within a fence or hedge. The colonists tend-

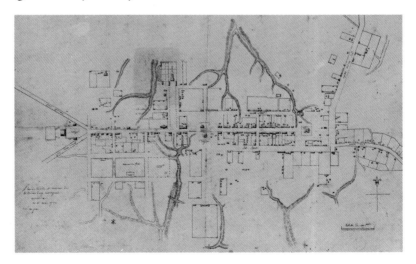

(Top to bottom)
The Reverend W. A. R. Goodwin (left) and John D. Rockefeller, Jr. Advertisement in the Virginia Gazette *(Purdie and Dixon), Dec. 16, 1773. The Frenchman's Map. Courtesy, Earl Gregg Swem Library, The College of William and Mary, Williamsburg, Va.*

ance. From the
very beginning,
Williamsburg's
restorers appre-
ciated the
importance of
reconstructing the gardens and
greens, as well as the houses and
shops.

When the restoration of
Williamsburg began, there was little
physical evidence remaining of eighteenth-century gardens. Here and
there, for instance, surviving bits of
holly and boxwood hedges suggested the bare bones of former garden
layouts. It was evident that considerable research would be necessary
to re-create the landscapes of the
colonial town. Vital research was
gathered from private and public
sources both in America and
abroad. Additional information per-
taining to the arrangement of gardens and outbuildings was revealed
through research into old tax
records and insurance policies,
which frequently included sketches
of the layout of lots. Descriptions of
the city occasionally appeared in the
surviving travelers' accounts, letters,
and journals. Explorers and natural-
ists also had kept detailed records of
plants found growing in Virginia
and neighboring colonies.

Archaeological excavations
were undertaken to locate buildings
and potential landscape features
such as outbuilding foundations,
brick and marl walks, paved service
areas, and old wall and fence lines.
In some cases, walkways uncovered
beneath the surface suggested the
former layout, including the garden
axis and the size, shape, and alignment of planting beds.

A number of surviving eighteenth-century maps have verified
the layout and growth of the town.

ed to create
the gardens
they remem-
bered, or their
parents
remembered,
in the En-
gland of
William and
Mary. Conse-
quently, these
styles persist-
ed longer in America where they
had been adopted than in England
where they had been fashioned.

The first gardens of any size or
consequence in Williamsburg were
at the College of William and Mary,
in "the college yard" at the east front
of the oldest structure, the Wren
Building. This decorative, formal
garden filled with topiary may have
looked out of place in the predomi-
nately natural landscape of Virginia,
but judging from surviving eyewit-
ness accounts, this was certainly an
appealing garden. This garden disappeared not long after the Revolutionary War.

The real greening of Williamsburg began when Lieutenant
Governor Alexander Spotswood
arrived in 1710. Embarking on a
path that would ultimately compromise his relationship with the
House of Burgesses, he undertook
at great expense the task of building

a monumental garden at the governor's mansion. For elegance and
extravagance, nothing in the colony
exceeded the governor's gardens,
and the reconstructed gardens have
been enormously influential in
telling the history of American
colonial gardening.

For Spotswood, gardens were
synonymous with civilized and elegant living, and his garden designs
were traditionally formal, geometric, and well balanced. This is the
conclusion we can draw from a cop-
perplate engraving discovered in
1929 by a Colonial Williamsburg
researcher in the Bodleian Library at
Oxford University, about 190 years
after it was originally executed. This
"Bodleian Plate" was of paramount
importance in guiding the garden
restoration efforts at the Palace.

RESTORATION OF
WILLIAMSBURG'S GARDENS
The story of the beginning of
Williamsburg's restoration is well
documented in the annals of the
American preservation movement.
In 1926, Dr. W. A. R. Goodwin,
then the rector of Bruton Parish
Church, was able to fire the imagi-
nation and enthusiasm of John D.
Rockefeller, Jr. Rockefeller agreed to
finance Dr. Goodwin's vision of
returning the city of Williamsburg
to its eighteenth-century appear-

The most useful has been the circa 1782 "Frenchman's Map," apparently drawn by a French officer for the purpose of billeting troops after the victory at Yorktown. In addition to showing streets and buildings accurately, this document provided detailed information about fence lines and delineates what appear to be trees at several locations.

Of primary importance during the early days of the restoration was the work of the Foundation's first landscape architect, Arthur A. Shurcliff, a pivotal figure in the development of the discipline of landscape architecture in America. Shurcliff was an internationally known landscape architect, uniquely qualified to play a leading role in the restoration. A resident of Boston, Shurcliff had studied under Frederick Law Olmsted, Sr., and helped to lay out the plans for Old Sturbridge Village in Massachusetts.

Shurcliff wrote that the re-created gardens were intended to "recall the period of the ancient dwellings and the old city itself." He quickly realized that local landscape traditions differed from those of other regions, as did the plants that were typically used. Much of his work was based on a careful, thorough study of surviving southern plantation homes and gardens, and of colonial Virginia gardens and homes in particular. Shurcliff's examination of some thirty-eight different colonial sites, combined with documented original garden designs, served as the precedents for the re-created gardens.

Through his research into colonial garden design, Shurcliff came to realize the value of the surviving eighteenth-century plans of North Carolina colonial towns and their gardens drawn by Claude Joseph Sauthier. Sauthier, a French landscape gardener who came to North Carolina in 1767, surveyed and drew plans for several of that colony's towns. Sauthier's plans included detailed renderings of intricate urban garden layouts, and established that their designs followed similar schemes and patterns typically seen in seventeenth-century English gardens. The style and pattern of these North Carolina gardens were Shurcliff's inspiration for several of Colonial Williamsburg's colonial revival gardens.

After World War I, a renewed interest by the American public in our colonial past began to give rise to the preservation of old homes and the veneration of all things "colonial." American history teaching became focused on the "Founding Fathers" with decidedly nationalistic and patriotic enthusiasm. Historic sites and house museums followed this trend, combining a unique blend of historical evidence and nostalgia to make the colonial past more appealing and attractive. This period has become known as "colonial revival" in the preservation movement as well as in decorative arts and design. Thus, these period gardens are considered to be colonial revival since they present a 1930s and 1940s view of our past created in spite of mounting evidence that most colonial gardens were simple, functional, and even somewhat bare.

Colonial Williamsburg bears the burden of criticism that the restored town appears too neat and clean, too "spick-and-span," and too manicured to be believable. In the beginning, Colonial Williamsburg was primarily an architectural restoration, and curatorial work at that time emphasized "high-style" design whether it be in decorative arts or garden design. Today, as a result of ongoing research, more emphasis is placed on social history showing how the colonists lived

(Top to bottom) Arthur A. Shurcliff. Shurcliff's plan for the Governor's Palace gardens. The Bryan House garden. A brick pier with an elegant stone finial in the gardens of the Governor's Palace.

(Left) Archaeological excavations in the Grissell Hay garden. (Right) Red spider lilies flank the path to the Benjamin Waller garden house.

and worked as a community. Williamsburg today is much more than a shrine to the pretty things of the past, and this thinking certainly now translates into how the gardens are currently presented. Colonial Williamsburg's Historic Area is a compromise between historical authenticity and common sense, between brutal realism and gentle ambience, between being a moment in time in the eighteenth century and being nearly three hundred years old.

Research into the gardens of Williamsburg has been actively pursued since the earliest days, and it continues today. Archaeological research techniques have changed dramatically, and little modern landscape archaeology has been completed in the Historic Area. New information continues to surface, often prompting a reconsideration of features of the town and its gardens.

WILLIAMSBURG GARDEN DESIGNS
There is no "typical" colonial Williamsburg garden. Then, as today, gardens were as varied as the people who created and tended them. The re-creation of a period garden is not a simple task. The actual trees, shrubs, and flowers that filled these gardens long ago have disappeared from the landscape, but we have clues as to how many of the

properties were laid out and the kinds of plants grown in the gardens. While these places are re-creations, they convey the spirit and character of the eighteenth century.

In many ways the organization of a property followed the dictates of the climate. Outbuildings seldom were connected to the house in this region where the winters are mild, and where the warm, humid summers make ample air circulation vital. The kitchen and each domestic service was usually given its own separate building with its own outside work space.

Probably most of Williamsburg's town gardens were the gardens of the colonial urban merchant or tradesmen classes with small backyard orchards and/or vegetable gardens planted with herbs and flowers scattered throughout. Secondary in importance and position to the kitchen yard, the garden was usually midway between the yard and the stable and paddock at the back of the property. As a general rule, service walks were laid to connect work areas in the most direct fashion, while the layout of walks in the gardens was typically geometric and balanced. "Necessary" houses, or privies, were usually located on a boundary of the garden—at the side or rear. There may have been a small orchard of fruit trees if space was available.

GARDEN FEATURES AND DETAILS
In surviving records there are only limited references to elaborate garden features or ornaments in Williamsburg's original gardens. From several sources, including

archaeological remains, there is evidence that the Governor's Palace gardens had elaborate gates, decorative vases, steps, seats, garden houses, and enclosing walls. Such decoration was rare in the smaller gardens that achieved interest with shrubs and colorful flowers. Little evidence has been found of lead figures or fountains such as those found in European gardens. Water as a garden feature, such a vital element in English gardens of the period, was virtually unknown in Williamsburg's gardens except at Governor Spotswood's canal and fish pond.

Fences, so commonly seen in Williamsburg today, were actually required by colonial law to be built around each lot. An act of the General Assembly of 1705, intended to protect the gardens from stray horses and cattle, required the owner of every lot on Duke of Gloucester Street to "inclose the said lots, or half acres, with a wall, pales, or post and rails, within six months after the building, which the law requires to be erected thereupon, shall be finished." The minimum height of the fence was set at four and one-half feet, and many were built higher. Brick walls with molded brick copings were not common around private houses but were usually confined to enclosing the grounds of public buildings.

Post and rail fences and picket fences were typical for private gardens. The "worm" or "snake" fence, frequently used to enclose fields in rural areas in and about Williamsburg, was made by laying rails in zigzag fashion without the need of posts. This was the ubiquitous "Virginia rail" fence which appeared as early as 1632 at Jamestown and continued in common use in Virginia until replaced

(Above) Elizabeth Carlos's house near Christiana Campbell's Tavern. (Right) Boxwood and topiary in the Greenhow Tenement garden near Market Square.

by the invention of barbed wire.

Work yards were often surfaced with a combination of materials including brick laid in patterns—basket weave, running bond, and herringbone—or in an irregular, crazy-quilt pattern of brickbats. Garden paths were commonly surfaced with marl or gravel. Brick and even crushed shells were occasionally used.

PLANTS IN COLONIAL GARDENS

By and large, the plants found in the gardens of Colonial Williamsburg are those native to the tidewater area or those introductions made by 1780. North America's contributions to the gardening world are chiefly its trees, flowering shrubs, and vines. American wildflowers have become essential perennials and annuals in flower borders around the world. The English colonists brought with them all manner of seeds, bulbs, and roots of their favorite flowers from back home, so their gardens became an amalgamation of those Old World favorites and the native plants they had found in the New World.

In the eighteenth century, the colonists carried on an extensive exchange of plants and horticultural information with the homeland. Much of what is known about plants available in Williamsburg's colonial times comes from correspondence about this exchange. John Custis, a prominent citizen of Williamsburg, corresponded for twelve years with Peter Collinson, the amateur English naturalist. Their letters are filled with the details of the joys and trials of the exchange of plants across the Atlantic. English gardeners were eager for the new American plants—exotics like black-eyed Susan, goldenrod, and the fall-blooming aster—that became popular in all of Europe. Likewise, literally hundreds of plants came to America from Europe. Some, like yarrow and daylily, escaped into the wild and have become thoroughly naturalized wildflowers of the American landscape. The majority of fruit trees, vegetables, herbs, and flowering bulbs came to Virginia from the Old World where they had been grown in English gardens for hundreds of years. Additionally, some vegetables native to Central and South America, such as potatoes and tomatoes, were introduced to North America and Virginia via Europe where Spanish and Portuguese explorers had taken them in the late fifteenth and sixteenth centuries.

There is still much research to be done on the history of ornamental plants grown in colonial Virginia gardens, for there will always be the source yet to be researched. References to plants in the seventeenth and eighteenth century are hampered by the unsystematic naming of plants before the Linnaean system of Latin genus and species names was established in 1753. Even more of a challenge is trying to match the proper genus and species names to the more colorful and unusual common names given to plants in colonial times. Since the planting of the first re-created gardens at Colonial Williamsburg, many plants have been added to the plant palette and more than a few have been deleted because of newly acquired information.

As summer days lengthen, Williamsburg's gardens, like other old Virginia gardens, take on a depth of greenness all their own. The source of this serenity is often the

boxwood, and it is the plant, above all others, that people typically associate with Williamsburg. Boxwood has proven itself the Virginia gardeners' best evergreen friend, withstanding winterkill and summer burn alike. While interesting when precisely trimmed in formal parterre gardens, boxwood is at its best when left to grow naturally into undulating and billowing masses.

Among the native ornamental trees available to gardeners of the eighteenth century were the dogwood, redbud, magnolia, and catalpa, all renowned for the beauty of their flowers. Commonly used trees that provided shade were the elm, chestnut, poplar, sycamore, oak, and pecan.

Fruit trees were very important in Williamsburg's early gardens. Fruits were eaten fresh, cooked, or preserved. The fruits of the Old World were in great demand and were usually grown in quantity. Fruits had been useful to the settlers of Virginia who found a natural bounty of grapes, and wild strawberries, huckleberries, blackberries, and raspberries that soon found their way into the garden. The native tree fruits proved to be less useful: the crab apple was small and bitter, the wild cherry was practically worthless, and the plum was inferior in quality to European varieties. The apple, quince, plum, pear, peach, cherry, apricot, and nectarine were all introduced from Europe.

In tribute to Williamsburg's

vegetable gardening heritage, we like to remember that John Randolph, a distinguished Virginian and resident of Williamsburg, wrote the first American book on kitchen or vegetable gardening. John Randolph was the king's attorney and was dubbed "John the Tory" because of his loyalist sympathies. Randolph's *Treatise on Gardening*, modeled on a similar manual by English nurseryman Philip Miller, was printed in America in 1788, four years after his death. Prior to that, only books written for English gardeners and the British climate had been available in the colonies, and thus provided little help with the particularities and peculiarities of this climate.

SUMMARY

The plants and re-created gardens in Williamsburg reflect the legacy of the early plantsmen. These colonial revival gardens, an important chapter in American garden history, have been enormously influential on garden design since the 1930s. These gardens capture the spirit and character of the finest eighteenth-century colonial gardens. Today, we face a reevaluation of many of these gardens, based on new research findings and techniques. Colonial Williamsburg's educational mission advocates that we go even further in re-creating noteworthy early gardens as more details become available. Where this is appropriate and well documented, changes will occur. With well-considered changes, we can depict more realistically what current research suggests is historically accurate. In the meantime, these beautiful green gardens will mature and grow more beautiful with each passing year.

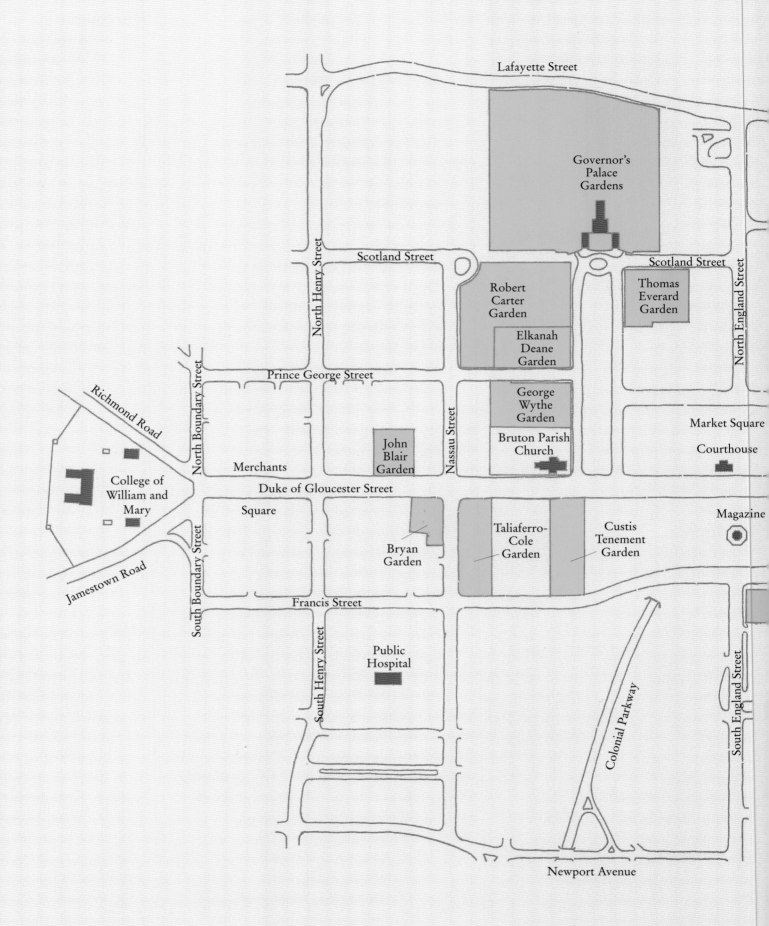

Lafayette Street

Governor's
Palace
Gardens

Scotland Street

Scotland Street

North Henry Street

North England Street

Robert
Carter
Garden

Thomas
Everard
Garden

Elkanah
Deane
Garden

Prince George Street

Richmond Road

North Boundary Street

George
Wythe
Garden

Nassau Street

Market Square

Courthouse

John
Blair
Garden

Bruton Parish
Church

Merchants

College of
William and
Mary

Duke of Gloucester Street

Square

Magazine

Taliaferro-
Cole
Garden

Custis
Tenement
Garden

Bryan
Garden

South Boundary Street

Jamestown Road

Francis Street

South Henry Street

Public
Hospital

Colonial Parkway

South England Street

Newport Avenue

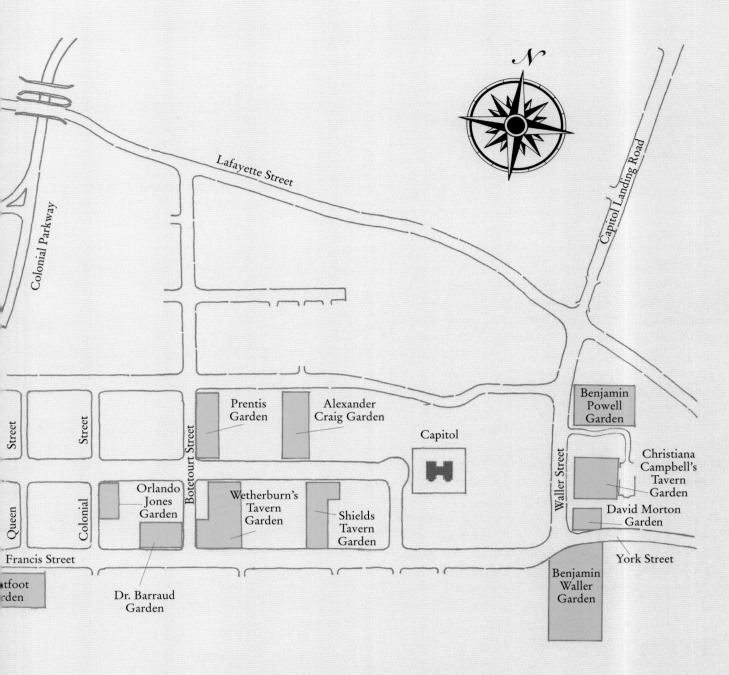

Lafayette Street

Colonial Parkway

Capitol Landing Road

Street

Street

Boteourt Street

Prentis Garden

Alexander Craig Garden

Capitol

Benjamin Powell Garden

Waller Street

Christiana Campbell's Tavern Garden

Queen

Colonial

Orlando Jones Garden

Wetherburn's Tavern Garden

Shields Tavern Garden

David Morton Garden

Francis Street

atfoot rden

Dr. Barraud Garden

York Street

Benjamin Waller Garden

THE GARDENS
OF COLONIAL WILLIAMSBURG

DR. BARRAUD HOUSE

The Dr. Barraud House at the intersection of Francis and Botetourt Streets is a surviving eighteenth-century dwelling and a splendid example of colonial architecture where symmetry rules. It is one of the few homes that face Francis Street on the north side since that side typically gives access to the backs of lots that front on Duke of Gloucester Street. The house reached its present configuration sometime before 1782 and incorporated an earlier structure. It was built by either William Carter, an apothecary, or James Anderson, the blacksmith who owned the property during the third quarter of the eighteenth century. Anderson lived on an adjacent lot and operated a blacksmith shop there.

Dr. Philip Barraud, along with Dr. John Minson Galt, was a visiting physician to the Public Hospital. By the 1780s, Barraud had purchased the house. He and his family lived there until 1799 when he went to Norfolk to become superintendent of the Portsmouth Marine Hospital. Barraud was a well-known public-spirited citizen active in affairs at the college.

THE DR. BARRAUD GARDEN
Dr. Barraud's garden, long a favorite with Williamsburg's visitors, incorporates three small, formal spaces and a natural, or wild, garden. Archaeological investigations on the site revealed foundations of several outbuildings, elaborate storm drains, brick pavements, and marl walks. In fact, the marl walks in the garden were some of the best preserved in Williamsburg, giving a clear indication of the garden's original layout. The configuration of the walkways revealed very definite relationships between the house, the outbuildings, and the garden areas that made it possible to envision the garden design. The privy is original, and three outbuildings, a kitchen, smokehouse, and wellhead, have been rebuilt on their original foundations.

The reconstructed garden is subdivided by fences into its component parts: one part kitchen yard, three parts formal garden, and one part natural garden. The kitchen yard, surfaced with marl and random brickbat paving, is dominated by a wellhead located on the site of the original household well. The simple fences and durable paving between the house and the kitchen provide a handy, spacious work yard.

The formal pleasure garden is composed of three small spaces of similar size. The most prominent of these is the grassy space west of the house accented with carefully sheared common boxwoods (*Buxus sempervirens*) and tall crape myrtles (*Lagerstroemia indica*). It is flanked with clipped boxwood hedges that separate it from the house and the small orchard to the west. A small sitting area with two benches completes the scene. The orchard, the second "compartment," is planted with apple trees (*Malus pumila*) and separated from the lower natural garden by a hedge of clipped yaupon hollies (*Ilex vomitoria*). Beyond these two spaces is the

(Right) The Dr. Barraud natural garden and (overleaf) the pleasure garden from the natural garden.

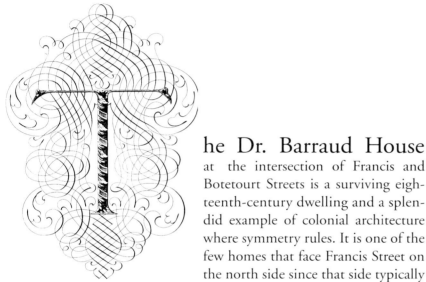

third element, a small flower garden planted with perennials, annuals, and bulbs with a garden bench at the west end. Since this rectangular space may have been the kitchen garden, it would have been considered a part of the kitchen yard.

The large tree shading the flower garden is a pink-flowering horse chestnut (*Aesculus X plantierensis*), with a second near the kitchen. Another rare plant, an American bladdernut (*Staphylea trifolia*), is located at the southwest corner of the kitchen. The native American bladdernut has rather insignificant green flowers but a most interesting seed capsule, a two-inch-long pale green inflated capsule that turns light brown in September. The bladdernut was cultivated in Virginia gardens as early as 1640.

The last part of the Barraud garden scheme is the lower "natural" garden that today resembles a wildflower garden set in a grove of trees. Most period terraced gardens had the flowers and ornamental plantings near the house while the lower levels were mainly for vegetables or herbs. So it is likely this area was a kitchen or vegetable garden. As the years passed, the vegetable garden was abandoned and a grove of trees evolved. The garden seen today was developed and maintained by a former occupant of the house, Mrs. Mary Ryland. Mrs. Ryland, who lived in this house until the early 1980s, planted the grove with ground covers and for many, many years set out numerous flowering bulbs in a helter-skelter fashion, resulting in the charming "wild" garden so appreciated by visitors. Depending on the season, you will find daffodils (*Narcissus Pseudonarcissus*), tulips (*Tulipa Gesnerana*), Dutch crocuses (*Crocus vernus*), Virginia bluebells (*Mertensia virginica*), windflowers (*Anemone coronaria*), and hyacinths (*Hyacinthus orientalis*). Mrs. Ryland's innovative garden scheme has been preserved in memory of this diligent Williamsburg gardener.

Research reveals that Dr. Barraud had a large vegetable garden across Francis Street in the vacant lot next to the Ewing House. The following excerpt of a letter written by St. George Tucker of Williamsburg in 1809 refers to this garden: "The other [property owned by Barraud] is a pretty good house on the same street, not so well situated and having, I believe about an acre of land across the street where Dr. Barraud, to whom it formerly belonged, had his garden . . ." Archaeological excavations corroborate this location. Apparently Barraud also used this garden area as a dump site because excavated trash pits contained fragments of initialed creamware that match fragments found adjacent to Barraud's house. Today, this site is planted in field crops such as clover or buckwheat.

A pink-flowering horse chestnut shades the kitchen yard.

Distinctively shaped pickets call attention to the fence surrounding the pleasure garden.

DR. BARRAUD HOUSE

PLANT LIST

TREES

1. Acer rubrum — Red maple
2. Aesculus X plantierensis — Pink-flowering horse chestnut
3. Aesculus Pavia — Red buckeye
4. Bumelia lanuginosa — Chittamwood
5. Carya illinoinensis — Pecan
6. Chionanthus virginicus — Old-man's-beard
7. Cornus florida — Flowering dogwood
8. Ilex opaca — American holly
9. Lagerstroemia indica — Crape myrtle
10. Morus alba — White mulberry
11. Prunus caroliniana — Cherry laurel
12. Prunus domestica — Common plum
13. Ulmus americana — American elm

SHRUBS

14. Buxus sempervirens — Common boxwood
15. Buxus sempervirens 'Suffruticosa' — Edging boxwood
16. Chaenomeles japonica — Flowering quince
17. Hibiscus syriacus — Rose-of-Sharon
18. Ilex vomitoria — Yaupon holly
19. Rosa sp. — Rose
20. Staphylea trifolia — American bladdernut
21. Syringa vulgaris — Common lilac
22. Viburnum dentatum — Southern arrowwood

VINES

23. Clematis virginiana — Virgin's bower
24. Gelsemium sempervirens — Carolina jessamine
25. Wisteria frutescens — American wisteria

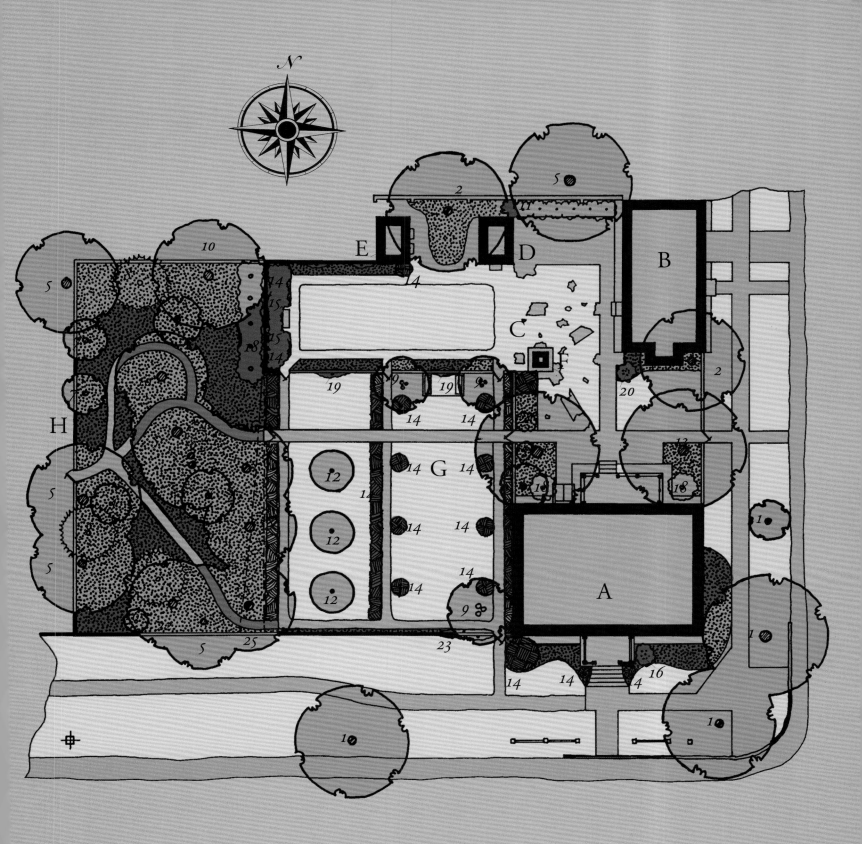

N

E

D

B

C

F

H

G

A

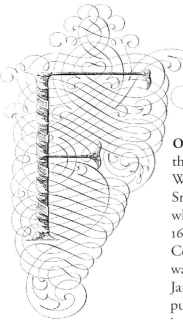

For more than a century the Blair family was associated with Williamsburg and Virginia. John Blair, Sr., was the son of Dr. Archibald Blair, who immigrated from Scotland about 1690. John Blair was educated at the College of William and Mary which was founded by his uncle, the Reverend James Blair. John Blair was a dedicated public servant. He served several years in the House of Burgesses and was appointed to the governor's Council in 1745, later becoming its president and twice serving as acting governor of the colony. John Blair, Sr., and his wife probably lived in this house for most of their married life, and he and his children continued to live here after his wife's death in 1750.

This is one of the oldest houses in Williamsburg. The east section of the John Blair House was built early in the eighteenth century and later lengthened twenty-eight feet to the west. The house is a splendid example of early Williamsburg architecture with hipped dormers and stone steps imported from England. Local tradition holds that the stone steps came from the Palace Street theater,

The kitchen dooryard garden features an assortment of fragrant herbs and colorful flowers.

the first theater established in English America. The house was restored in 1929, one of the first to be completed under the then modest restoration project. The wellhead, woodshed, and smokehouse were reconstructed on their original, though fragmentary, foundations. The kitchen with its huge chimney was reconstructed in 1937 with the adjacent herb garden.

THE JOHN BLAIR GARDEN

Through much of his lifetime John Blair, Sr., kept a diary in which he recorded his love of gardening. In February 1751, Blair noted in his diary that his gardener had "fought with someone else's," and in May he had loaned his gardener to Peyton Randolph, of whom "Mrs. Randolph gave a fine account." However, by June he recorded that he "ordered the gardener to go, for I couldn't bear him." In November, he "planted flowers," obtained orange trees from the Green Spring plantation nursery, and mentioned "fine greens" for dinner that came from his garden.

The yard directly behind the house is a small orchard featuring peaches (*Prunus Persica*), apples (*Malus pumila*), and sour cherries (*Prunus Cerasus*). Surrounding the orchard is an unusual clipped hedge of American beeches (*Fagus grandifolia*) backed by a tall wooden fence. The small tree near the kitchen is an American hornbeam (*Carpinus caroliniana*), a splendid native understory tree with a spreading habit.

The kitchen dooryard is a small herb garden, reminiscent of the "physick" gardens popular in the seventeenth century. Landscape architect Arthur A. Shurcliff designed the garden with a series of narrow walks dividing the forty- by fifty-foot area into two sections, each with a central diamond-shaped parterre accented within a clipped yaupon holly (*Ilex vomitoria*). The parterres are filled with an ever-changing assortment of annual and biennial flowers and perennial herbs, both culinary and medicinal. The raised brick edging allows for a narrower walk as well as for neater and easier maintenance. Enclosure for this small garden is provided by the buildings on the north, the surrounding yaupon holly hedge, and the picket fences. The walk behind the hedge next to the kitchen is raised one step, permitting a better view of the intricate garden design.

(Above and right) The reconstructed smokehouse is a quaint backdrop to this rigidly formal garden of parterres and narrow brick walks.

The reconstructed smokehouse.

Rosa Mundi rose.

Pot marigolds.

Damask rose.

Foxgloves and candytufts line the walk.

A clipped yaupon holly hedge.

Apothecary's roses.

Foxgloves.

Dame's rocket and pot marigolds.

PLANT LIST FOR THE HERB GARDEN

STRUCTURAL/FOUNDATION PLANTS IN THE HERB GARDEN

1. Allium Schoenoprasum — Chives
2. Ilex vomitoria — Yaupon holly
3. Rosa chinensis 'Old Blush' — Old blush rose
4. Rosa damascena — Damask rose
5. Rosa gallica officinalis — Apothecary's rose
6. Rosa gallica 'Versicolor' — Rosa Mundi rose
7. Rosmarinus officinalis — Rosemary
8. Thymus vulgaris — Common thyme

P—PERENNIAL AND SEASONAL FLOWERS AND HERBS

Agastache Foeniculum	Anise hyssop
Aloysia triphylla	Lemon verbena
Anthemis nobilis	Chamomile
Artemisia Abrotanum	Southernwood
Artemisia Absinthium	Absinthe
Centranthus ruber	Red valerian
Chrysanthemum Balsamita	Costmary
Chrysanthemum coccineum	Pyrethum
Chrysanthemum parthenium	Feverfew
Centaurea moschata	Sweet-sultan
Convallaria majalis	Lily-of-the-valley
Dianthus Caryophyllus	Clove pink
Hemerocallis fulva	Tawny daylily
Hyssopus officinalis	Hyssop
Iberis sempervirens	Edging candytuft
Iris X germanica var. florentina	Orris
Lavandula angustifolia subsp. angustifolia	English lavender
Lilium candidum	Madonna lily

Melissa officinalis	Lemon balm
Mentha Pulegium	Pennyroyal
Mentha spicata	Spearmint
Monarda didyma	Bee balm
Myrtus communis	Myrtle
Nepeta Cataria	Catnip
Origanum vulgare	Marjoram
Pelargonium X domesticum	Lady Washington geranium
Pelargonium crispum	Lemon geranium
Pelargonium graveolens	Rose geranium
Pelargonium quercifolium	Oak-leaved geranium
Pycnanthemum pilosum	Mountain mint
Ruta graveolens	Common rue
Salvia Sclarea	Clary sage
Santolina Chamaecyparissus	Lavender cotton
Santolina virens	Green lavender cotton
Tanacetum vulgare	Common tansy
Valeriana officinalis	Common valerian
Viola odorata	Sweet violet

A—ANNUAL AND SEASONAL FLOWERS AND HERBS

Asphodeline lutea	Asphodel
Calendula officinalis	Pot marigold
Cheiranthus Cheiri	English wallflower
Dianthus barbatus	Sweet William
Dianthus chinensis	Rainbow pink
Digitalis purpurea	Common foxglove
Hesperis matronalis	Dame's rocket
Matthiola incana	Stock
Myosotis sylvatica	Garden forget-me-not
Narcissus Jonquilla	Jonquil
Nicotiana alata	Flowering tobacco
Reseda odorata	Common mignonette
Tropaeolum majus	Garden nasturtium

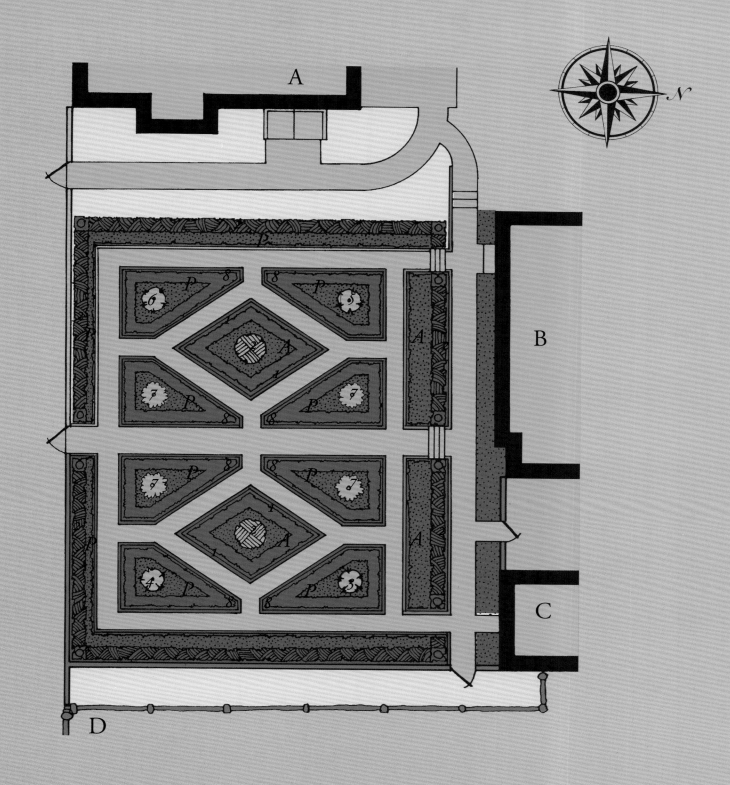

JOHN BLAIR HOUSE

KEY TO THE PLAN

A. John Blair House
B. Kitchen

C. Smokehouse
D. Pasture

(Left) Red valerian, dame's rocket, chives, and foxgloves.

THOMAS EVERARD HOUSE

The property is known for two residents, John Brush, an early eighteenth-century gunsmith, and Thomas Everard, a noted public official and colonial mayor of Williamsburg. John Brush, a gunsmith known for his craftsmanship in England, acquired this property in 1717 and built a simple house shortly thereafter. By about 1755, Thomas Everard had purchased the front sections of the lot; he bought the rear in 1773. Everard served for nearly forty years as clerk of York County, was twice elected mayor of Williamsburg, and served as clerk of the House of Burgesses' Committee of Courts of Justice.

The Frenchman's Map of 1782 locates six structures on this site. In addition to the house, the kitchen is original and restored. Brick paving and surface drains were found behind the house during archaeological excavations. The paving next to the house was about twelve inches below the present grade and laid in rows. The walkway leading toward the east, centered on the boxwood garden, was laid with brickbats in a crazy-quilt design. A similar four-foot-wide walk of brickbats laid over a marl base ran west from the kitchen to the gate near the street. Several layers of marl paths were found at the front of the house and around the north side.

THE THOMAS EVERARD GARDEN
The Thomas Everard site has two distinctive garden styles, naturalistic and formal, in a beautiful setting of pond, grass, and ancient boxwoods. This property offers the opportunity to ponder influences of both formal and natural English landscape design patterns on the colonies in the eighteenth century. The formal garden behind the house and the informal garden around the pond illustrate the contrast. While naturalistic designs did not become popular in this country until the mid-nineteenth century, there were those in the late eighteenth century who favored the new, modern style. At both Monticello and Mount Vernon, Thomas Jefferson and George Washington laid out their walkways and drives in the natural, informal manner.

There has been much speculation concerning the age, and who might have planted, the old boxwood (*Buxus sempervirens 'Suffruticosa'*) garden east of the house. Analysis suggests that the oldest of these boxwoods were planted about 1830. At that time the house was well over one hundred years old, and it certainly is possible that today's ancient boxwoods were replacements to a hedge that bordered the central garden walk. Archaeologists determined that the old marl walkway, now completely covered over by the rambling boxwoods, was put in late in the eighteenth century.

The boxwood garden has been preserved, but the garden today is probably quite a bit different from its eighteenth-century appearance. Prior to 1773, the garden was smaller since the rear property line was just beyond the two privies, so an expansion of the garden would likely have occurred when Everard purchased the rear lot. This was probably when the central garden path was built, but we can only speculate about the boxwoods and the former garden. Nonetheless, the garden is a remarkable survival from the past.

(Right) The pleasure garden filled with mature edging boxwood, some of the oldest boxwood in Williamsburg's gardens.

The house and the kitchen are framed by ancient boxwood and a grove of American hornbeam in this view from the garden.

PLANT LIST

TREES

1. Acer saccharinum — Silver maple
2. Acer rubrum — Red maple
3. Carpinus caroliniana — American hornbeam
4. Celtis occidentalis — Sugarberry
5. Cercis canadensis — Redbud
6. Cornus florida — Flowering dogwood
7. Forestiera acuminata — Swamp privet
8. Ilex opaca — American holly
9. Juglans nigra — Black walnut
10. Lagerstroemia indica — Crape myrtle
11. Magnolia grandiflora — Southern magnolia
12. Malus coronaria — Wild sweet crab apple
13. Mespilus germanica — Medlar
14. Morus alba — White mulberry
15. Prunus caroliniana — Cherry laurel
16. Quercus falcata — Spanish red oak
17. Quercus laurifolia — Laurel oak
18. Quercus virginiana — Southern live oak
19. Robinia Pseudoacacia — Black locust

22. Chaenomeles speciosa — Flowering quince
23. Ficus carica — Common fig
24. Ilex vomitoria — Yaupon holly
25. Myrica cerifera — Wax myrtle
26. Philadelphus coronarius — Mock orange
27. Prunus glandulosa — Flowering almond
28. Punica Granatum — Pomegranate
29. Rhus aromatica — Fragrant sumac
30. Rosa laevigata — Cherokee rose
31. Rosa species — Rose
32. Rosa spinosissima — Scotch rose
33. Syringa Josikaea — Hungarian lilac
34. Viburnum dentatum — Southern arrowwood
35. Viburnum Lentago — Nannyberry
36. Viburnum Opulus — Cranberry bush
37. Viburnum prunifolium — Black haw
38. Vitex Agnus-castus — Chaste tree
39. Vitex negundo var. 'heterophylla' — Cutleaf chaste tree

SHRUBS

20. Amelanchier canadensis — Shadbush
21. Buxus sempervirens 'Suffruticosa' — Edging boxwood

VINES

40. Celastrus scandens — American bittersweet

THOMAS EVERARD HOUSE

KEY TO THE PLAN

A. Thomas Everard House
B. Office
C. Smokehouse
D. Kitchen
E. Laundry
F. Dairy and Well
G. Stable
H. Privies
I. Door Yard
J. Pleasure Garden
K. Pond

BRYAN HOUSE

T he Bryan House and elaborate side garden occupy a prominent position on Duke of Gloucester Street near Merchants Square. The frame house dates to the mid-1700s and survived into the early twentieth century. Research on this site has been hampered by the destruction during the Civil War of the James City County records. The Frenchman's Map indicates a large structure directly on the street corner, with several outbuildings to the rear along the side street. Other maps, also prior to 1800, show William Bryan owning this lot, and the land tax records substantiate this record. Late nineteenth-century photographs and descriptions by residents who recalled the appearance of the house aided efforts in reconstruction.

During archaeological excavations near the kitchen, foundations of a building located partially in the street were discovered. That building faced on the early seventeenth-century path that preceded the settlement of Williamsburg in 1699. Possibly due to the early history of habitation on this site, the west and south fence lines are angled, unlike the majority of property lines in Williamsburg. During reconstruction, the irregular shape of the lot was established by postholes found that corresponded to fence lines shown on the Frenchman's Map. Archaeological investigations and other old maps substantiate this property line alignment.

Dwarf fruit trees and boxwood topiaries highlight the richly varied Bryan House garden.

THE BRYAN GARDEN

This colonial revival garden was based on garden patterns depicted on Sauthier's maps of North Carolina towns of about 1769. The kitchen yard is a generous brick-paved area connecting the house, kitchen, smokehouse, and well in a typical arrangement. Now shaded by a crape myrtle (*Lagerstroemia indica*), the yard displays several different kinds of brick paving: random brickbat, basket weave, and running bond patterns. This work yard not only has immediate and convenient access to the side street but to other parts of the property as well.

To the south, beyond the kitchen yard, lies what was once a kitchen garden. Now planted in grass, it probably would have been planted in vegetables, flowers, and herbs for household use. Crosswalks divide the space into planting areas, and a side gate gives access to the rear of the pleasure garden. The stable is on the south property line, and the former paddock is used for resident parking. Majestic, though weedy, trees-of-heaven (*Ailanthus altissima*) line the east side of Nassau Street.

The Bryan garden is unusual because it has no axial orientation to the rear of the house. Instead, it is placed to one side, an orientation it shares with several other Williamsburg properties: Christiana Campbell's Tavern, Benjamin Powell House, Alexander Craig House, and Custis Tenement. Each of these gardens is directly accessible from the street, and the house can be reached only through the service yard or by other indirect paths.

Brick paths divide the pleasure, or parterre, garden into eight planting beds, each symmetrically placed around a central square. The four central parterres are planted with English ivy (*Hedera Helix*) and spring-flowering bulbs. But like most geometric parterres, the beauty of this garden lies not in its two-dimensional arrangement of squares and rectangles but in its three-dimensional forms: clipped apple (*Malus pumila*) trees arranged within a frame of clipped boxwood hedging. While this combination is pleasing, it was more common in garden plans of this period to find fruit trees planted in separate orchards rather than in parterre gardens.

A dahoon holly (*Ilex Cassine*) is the featured plant in the central parterre and provides a large, dominant, vertical accent in the middle of the garden. Dahoon is a native evergreen shrub or small tree typically found in swampy areas in the southeast United States.

An arbor covered with trumpet honeysuckles

(Above) A view of the garden in the winter.
(Right) The brilliant color of a crape myrtle in an adjacent garden dominates the precision of the boxwood hedges and carefully trimmed topiaries.

Flanked by four boxwood topiaries, a native dahoon holly is the featured plant in the Bryan House garden.

(*Lonicera sempervirens*) and American wisterias (*Wisteria frutescens*) offers a cool, shady retreat with a splendid view of the garden. Along the street, the picket fence is blanketed with a Cherokee rose (*Rosa laevigata*). The Cherokee rose, native to China, was introduced into European gardens in the mid-1700s.

The garden gate is shaded by the unusual medlar tree (*Mespilus germanica*), and beds of tree peonies (*Paeonia suffruticosa*) flank the walk. In the early spring, a large cornelian cherry (*Cornus mas*) with its masses of fragrant yellow flowers dominates the northeast corner of the garden near the house.

BRYAN HOUSE

PLANT LIST

TREES

1. Acer rubrum — Red maple
2. Ailanthus altissima — Tree-of-heaven
3. Celtis occidentalis — Sugarberry
4. Cornus florida — Flowering dogwood
5. Cornus mas — Cornelian cherry
6. Fagus grandifolia — American beech
7. Juniperus virginiana — Red cedar
8. Lagerstroemia indica — Crape myrtle
9. Liriodendron Tulipifera — Tulip poplar
10. Magnolia virginiana — Sweet bay
11. Malus pumila — Common apple
12. Mespilus germanica — Medlar
13. Prunus domestica — Common plum
14. Quercus phellos — Willow oak
15. Ulmus americana — American elm

SHRUBS

16. Buxus sempervirens — Common boxwood
17. Calycanthus floridus — Carolina allspice
18. Ficus carica — Common fig
19. Ilex Cassine — Dahoon holly
20. Ilex vomitoria — Yaupon holly
21. Myrica cerifera — Wax myrtle
22. Paeonia suffruticosa — Tree peony
23. Philadelphus coronarius — Mock orange
24. Prunus caroliniana — Cherry laurel
25. Rosa laevigata — Cherokee rose
26. Syringa vulgaris — Common lilac
27. Vitex Negundo var. 'heterophylla' — Cutleaf chaste tree

VINES

28. Lonicera sempervirens — Trumpet honeysuckle
29. Wisteria frutescens — American wisteria

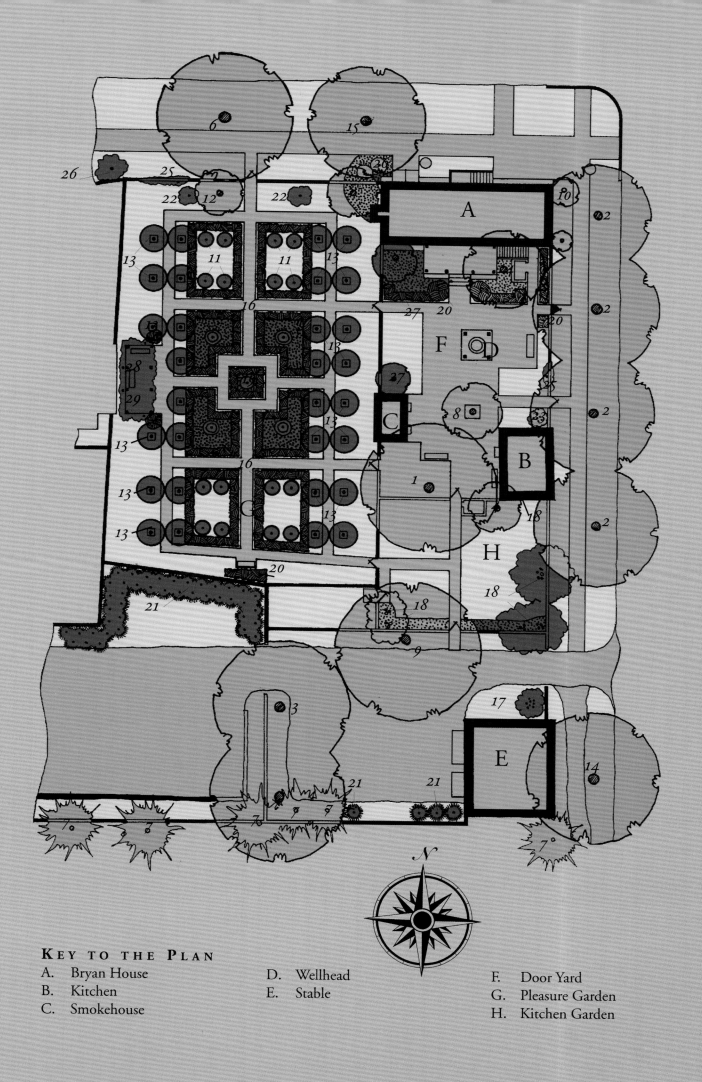

KEY TO THE PLAN

A. Bryan House
B. Kitchen
C. Smokehouse

D. Wellhead
E. Stable

F. Door Yard
G. Pleasure Garden
H. Kitchen Garden

CHRISTIANA CAMPBELL'S TAVERN

In addition to eating, drinking, and gaming, in the eighteenth century Christiana Campbell's Tavern had rooms to rent and a stable for horses. The tavern's proximity to the Capitol undoubtedly contributed to its success. Early in the eighteenth century, the entire area east of the Capitol was the property of Mann Page, a Gloucester County landowner. In 1749, Benjamin Waller purchased much Waller Street property from Page. Waller owned the property where Campbell's now stands until 1751, when he sold the lots to Alexander Finnie. The sales agreement provided that within three years Finnie would build "2 good Dwelling Houses . . . at least with Brick Chimneys," or the property would revert back to Waller. Fulfilling those conditions proved to be difficult for a succession of owners. By the mid-1760s, there was a tavern on the site operated by Jane Vobe until 1771 and by Christiana Campbell from 1771 to about 1785.

Christiana Campbell had a long history of tavern keeping; in fact, it was a family tradition. Her father was John Burdett, who operated a tavern on the other side of the Capitol on Duke of Gloucester Street. When widowed, Campbell began keeping a tavern and ran one of the most popular of the many public houses in Williamsburg. On occasion, she hosted George Washington, who was said to have been one of her most frequent customers during his Williamsburg visits.

An overview of Christiana Campbell's Tavern garden featuring a yaupon holly topiary flanked by gold-dust plants.

THE CAMPBELL'S TAVERN GARDEN

Excavations of the tavern in 1950 and the outbuildings and kitchen in 1953 confirmed much that had been gleaned from other documentary evidence. One insurance policy mentions the building having a brick underpinning two feet above the ground, a cellar, a kitchen twenty feet by sixteen, and a blacksmith shop. Thomas Sands, owner in 1801, described the property as "two buildings facing the main street back of the Capitol at Williamsburg . . . wood dwelling . . . wood kitchen."

The only documented mention of a garden associated with this property is in the deed between John Stretch and Alexander Finnie in April 1757 that described the purchase "with all Houses . . . and Gardens . . ."

Although there seems to be little precedent for a formal garden in this spot, and no archaeological evidence to justify the location or the design, landscape architect Alden Hopkins designed a beautiful colonial revival garden beside the tavern. The geometric pattern features nine planting beds: four square beds notched on the inside corners to accommodate a central circle planted with a tiered topiary yaupon holly (*Ilex vomitoria*), and four rectangular beds, two on the west and two on the east side of the garden, planted with English ivy (*Hedera Helix*). A flowering dogwood (*Cornus florida*) in each of the eight rectangular beds provides a soft canopy and shelter from the sun for the gold-dust trees (*Aucuba japonica Variegata*) that accent the four central squares.

The garden seems to bear an aspect of great age because of the eight huge cedars that create the illusion of sheer green walls around three sides. The contrast between the vertical red cedars (*Juniperus virginiana*) and the patterns of the precisely edged parterres is mediated by the middling height of the nearly mature dogwoods. In midsummer, another beautiful contrast occurs between the yellow-and-green variegated foliage of the gold-dust trees and the underplantings of creeping St.-John's-wort (*Hypericum calycinum*) with golden yellow blossoms. In autumn, the garden rebounds with color when the dogwoods turn deep russet and when the oakleaf hydrangeas (*Hydrangea quercifolia*) turn nearly the same color with browning panicles.

PLANT LIST

TREES

1.	Acer rubrum	Red maple
2.	Cercis canadensis	Redbud
3.	Cornus florida	Flowering dogwood
4.	Juniperus virginiana	Red cedar
5.	Melia Azedarach	Chinaberry
6.	Prunus Cerasus 'Montmorency'	Montmorency cherry
7.	Pyrus communis	Common pear
8.	Quercus falcata	Spanish red oak
9.	Quercus phellos	Willow oak
10.	Ulmus americana	American elm

SHRUBS

11.	Aucuba japonica Variegata	Gold-dust tree
12.	Buxus sempervirens	Common boxwood
13.	Buxus sempervirens 'Suffruticosa'	Edging boxwood
14.	Chimonanthus praecox	Wintersweet
15.	Clethra alnifolia	Summer-sweet
16.	Hydrangea quercifolia	Oakleaf hydrangea
17.	Ilex vomitoria	Yaupon holly
18.	Lonicera tatarica	Tatarian honeysuckle
19.	Myrica cerifera	Wax myrtle
20.	Philadelphus coronarius	Mock orange
21.	Punica Granatum	Pomegranate
22.	Rhus aromatica	Fragrant sumac
23.	Rosa virginiana	Virginia rose
24.	Syringa persica	Persian lilac
25.	Vitex Agnus-castus	Chaste tree
26.	Yucca filamentosa	Adam's-needle

VINES

27.	Bignonia capreolata	Cross vine
28.	Celastrus scandens	American bittersweet
29.	Gelsemium sempervirens	Carolina jessamine
30.	Lonicera sempervirens	Trumpet honeysuckle
31.	Wisteria sinensis	Chinese wisteria

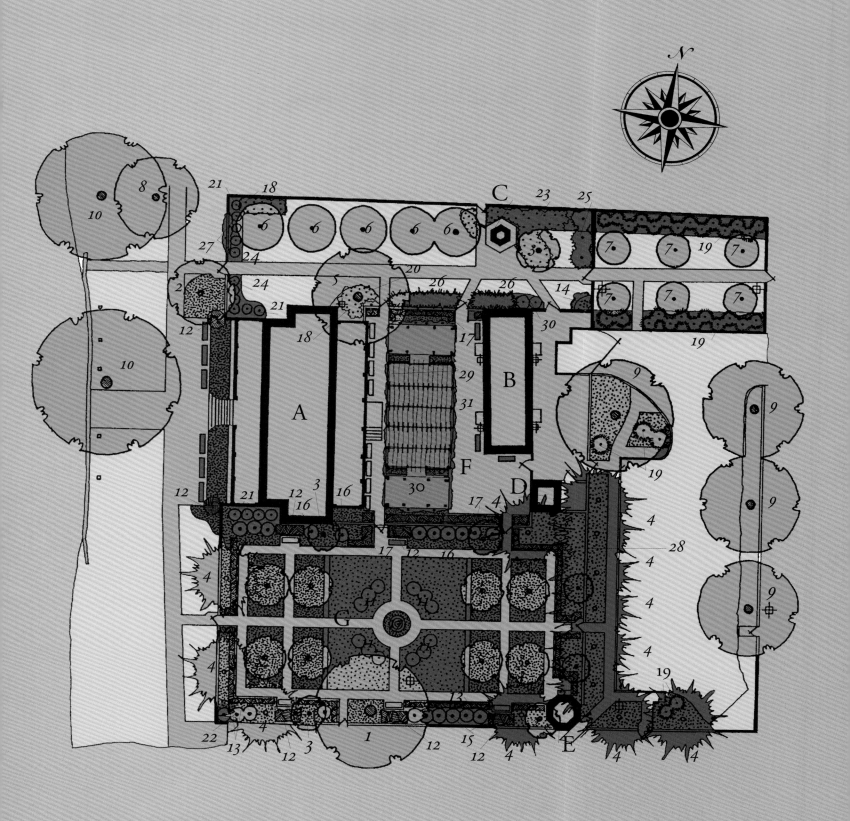

CHRISTIANA CAMPBELL'S TAVERN

KEY TO THE PLAN

A. Christiana Campbell's Tavern
B. Quarters
C. Well
D. Smokehouse
E. Privy
F. Outdoor Dining
G. Pleasure Garden

This large, rambling frame house adjacent to the Palace on the west side of Palace green is one of the most impressive in Williamsburg. Situated on four half-acre lots, with the exception of the Governor's Palace, it is one of the largest domestic properties in the city and includes the original residence, an original brick quarters, and a complex of reconstructed outbuildings.

This property was acquired by Charles Carter, a son of Robert "King" Carter, one of the wealthiest planters in colonial Virginia, prior to 1746. In 1747, Dr. Kenneth McKenzie purchased the property and lived with his family in the house. It was Dr. McKenzie who built the apothecary shop on Palace Street.

In 1751, a committee of the Council purchased the home as a temporary residence for the governor while repairs were made to the official residence. Thus Lieutenant Governor Robert Dinwiddie and his family moved into the house in November and lived there for about a year.

The next owner was yet another member of the Carter family, Robert Carter Nicholas, who purchased the property in 1753. Needing more room for his growing family, he sold the house in 1761 to his cousin, Robert Carter III of Nomini Hall in Westmoreland County. This family of Carters also outgrew the house and returned to Nomini Hall in 1772. After attempting to sell the property, Carter rented it to several different tenants and caretakers through the years.

When Colonial Williamsburg acquired this property in 1928, archaeological evidence of the eighteenth-century condition was confused by so many alterations and additions that a complete restoration and reconstruction was difficult. Though the archaeological techniques then in use were crude by today's standards, they did enable

The McKenzie Apothecary (left) and Robert Carter House (right) from the Palace green.

the discovery of fence lines, brick walkways, wells, and building foundations. With the removal of numerous alterations (with the exception of the back porch), the house was restored to its eighteenth-century appearance. Except for the original brick quarters that were restored, all the outbuildings are reconstructions on their original foundations.

THE ROBERT CARTER GARDEN

References to gardening activities on the part of the Saunders family in the nineteenth century hint at surviving gardens or a continuing gardening tradition dating from the eighteenth century. The terraces, or "falls," behind the house are considered to be eighteenth-century features. Although badly eroded, the turf ramps have been repaired and are today one of the prominent and beautiful features of the re-created landscape.

The landscape plan devised by landscape architect Arthur A. Shurcliff was simple in its overall treatment of the site. An ornate, formal flower garden with topiary boxwoods (*Buxus sempervirens*) and parterres was located at the north end of the terraced area. Subsequent archaeological investigations revealed the foundations of a dairy that had been overlooked in the first reconstruction efforts. The formal parterre garden was removed since the presence of this garden was conjectural in the first place, and the discovery of the dairy confirmed that this had been a service area rather than a pleasure garden.

The front of the house has a restrained landscape treatment. The entrance is flanked by crape myrtles (*Lagerstroemia indica*), and running the length of the house are beds of English ivy (*Hedera Helix*) interplant-ed with bulbs. Along the covered walkway beside the sidewalk is a paper mulberry tree (*Broussonetia papyrifera*) replacing an older, gnarled one which stood at that location for generations. At the corner of the adjacent apothecary shop is a chaste tree (*Vitex Agnus-castus*). The chaste tree, a spreading aromatic shrub native to the Mediterranean region, has been cultivated in English gardens since 1570.

In this lovely setting are numerous varieties of trees including redbud (*Cercis canadensis*), dogwood (*Cornus florida*), southern live oak (*Quercus virginiana*), black walnut (*Juglans nigra*), sugarberry (*Celtis occidentalis*), American elm (*Ulmus americana*), American holly (*Ilex opaca*), old-man's beard (*Chionanthus virginicus*), cherry laurel (*Prunus caroliniana*), and osage orange (*Maclura pomifera*). The osage orange, a member of the mulberry family and native to the Mississippi River valley, is only occasionally grown in Williamsburg's gardens since it reportedly was introduced into cultivation as a result of the Meriwether Lewis and William Clark expedition of 1804–1806.

Boxwoods (*Buxus sempervirens*) and gold-dust trees (*Aucuba japonica Variegata*) are found near the back porch, roses-of-Sharon (*Hibiscus syriacus*) near the brick quarters, and American hazelnuts (*Corylus americana*) around the dairy. Plantings of wax myrtles (*Myrica cerifera*) and English ivy (*Hedera Helix*) on the bank surrounding the privy help to provide a discreet screen.

(Above) The house has a commanding view of the garden terraces, here seen from the south orchard. (Left) The main garden terrace and the kitchen.

The North Well is convenient to the Brick Quarters through a yaupon hedge with clipped accents.

ROBERT CARTER HOUSE

KEY TO THE PLAN

A. Robert Carter House
B. Kitchen
C. Office
D. McKenzie Apothecary
E. Brick Quarters
F. Meat House
G. North Well
H. South Well
I. Poultry House
J. Dairy
K. Privy
L. Chariot House
M. Stable
N. Sheep Shelter
O. Kitchen Yard
P. Garden
Q. North Orchard
R. South Orchard
S. Pasture

PLANT LIST

TREES

1.	Aesculus Pavia	Red buckeye
2.	Broussonetia papyrifera	Paper mulberry
3.	Catalpa speciosa	Western catawba
4.	Celtis occidentalis	Sugarberry
5.	Cercis canadensis	Redbud
6.	Cornus florida 'rubra'	Pink-flowering dogwood
7.	Corylus americana	American hazelnut
8.	Ilex opaca	American holly
9.	Juglans nigra	Black walnut
10.	Lagerstroemia indica	Crape myrtle
11.	Maclura pomifera	Osage orange
12.	Malus coronaria	Wild sweet crab apple
13.	Morus alba	White mulberry
14.	Platanus occidentalis	Eastern sycamore
15.	Prunus caroliniana	Cherry laurel
16.	Prunus Persica	Peach
17.	Quercus laurifolia	Laurel oak
18.	Quercus virginiana	Southern live oak
19.	Salix nigra	Black willow
20.	Ulmus americana	American elm
21.	Ulmus procera	English elm

SHRUBS

22.	Aucuba japonica Variegata	Gold-dust tree
23.	Buxus sempervirens	Common boxwood
24.	Buxus sempervirens 'Suffruticosa'	Edging boxwood
25.	Chaenomeles speciosa	Flowering quince
26.	Ilex vomitoria	Yaupon holly
27.	Myrica cerifera	Wax myrtle
28.	Rosa spinosissima	Scotch rose
29.	Syringa vulgaris	Common lilac
30.	Vitex Agnus-castus	Chaste tree

VINES

31.	Campsis radicans	Trumpet creeper

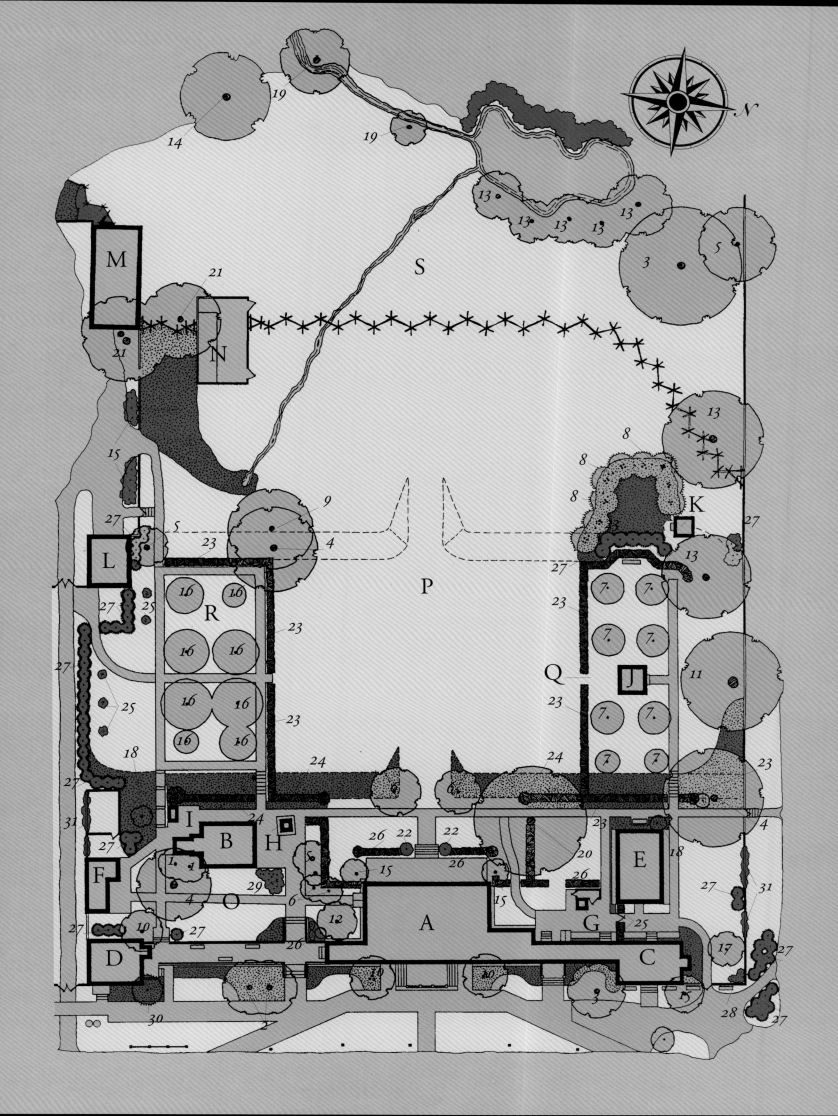

ALEXANDER CRAIG HOUSE

s with so many buildings in the eighteenth-century capital, the Alexander Craig House had a multitude of owners, and as many different types of businesses operated on the premises. This restored dwelling with attached shop and adjoining garden is located next to the Raleigh Tavern site near the Capitol. The east end of Duke of Gloucester Street had a greater concentration of commercial establishments than quieter parts of the city. This property was very much a part of the business bustle and activity, serving first as a tavern, next a wig shop, and, from 1771, as the combined house and shop of the Craig family.

The house was built about 1735 on the eastern section of the lot originally owned by John Peter Wagnon, a wigmaker. Wagnon sold the property shortly afterward to Andrew Anderson, another wigmaker, who operated a wig shop there for a number of years. In 1755, Alexander Craig acquired the east section of the property, and by 1771 he had purchased the west section, all the while plying his trade as a saddle- and harnessmaker. He died in 1776, and by 1782 the property was owned by Dr. John Minson Galt, Craig's son-in-law, who was conducting business as an apothecary and surgeon in his shop two doors to the east.

Like many Williamsburg dwellings, this one and one-half story house grew in stages, which accounts for its individuality and charm. Research points to several additions having been made during the 1700s. The last was the long shed roof on the rear.

A simple garden gate is flanked by boxwood topiaries and fronted with single late tulips in a mixture of colors.

THE ALEXANDER CRAIG GARDEN

Gardens and outbuildings were mentioned in the recorded deeds for the property, but little is known of their actual appearance. The brick walks in the orchard were discovered, intact, during the archaeological investigations. These old brick walks are badly worn and awkward to use; therefore, the main path is now covered over with a wooden boardwalk for safety. Elsewhere in the orchard, the original brickbat paths have been left uncovered so the original pattern and condition can be seen.

The Alexander Craig garden was developed at one side of the property rather than behind the house as was more typical. Because the garden fronts onto the street, a unique view of the series of "garden rooms" that make up the Craig garden can be enjoyed by the casual stroller without actually entering the garden. The site slopes gently away from the street elevation accenting the linearity of the entire garden.

The first division of the garden, or the first garden room, begins with a simple garden bench set in a

bed of English ivy (*Hedera Helix*). From this comfortable point of view, the flanking four-foot hedges of clipped common boxwoods (*Buxus sempervirens*) lead the eye on to the next garden space, the parterre garden, and then on through to the third space, the grassy orchard crisscrossed with brick walks. The eye then comes to rest at one of two arbors of clipped American hornbeams (*Carpinus caroliniana*) set beneath the dark, waxy boughs of two enormous southern magnolias (*Magnolia grandiflora*). The vista is further accentuated by a pair of sweet bays (*Magnolia virginiana*) planted at the north end of each boxwood hedge, which frame the view of the succeeding gardens.

The second garden room, the parterre garden, is a rectangular space, surrounded with common box-

(Above) Single late tulips provide a pleasing foreground to this view of the Raleigh Tavern dependencies. (Above right) A cone-shaped boxwood accents the circular bed of marigolds. (Right) Purple cockscombs highlight this same bed another year.

woods, featuring four similarly shaped parterres arranged around a circular bed. The four parterres are edged in English lavender (*Lavandula angustifolia subsp. angustifolia*). English lavender is an aromatic Old World perennial and member of the mint family. Usually found in the herb garden and chiefly grown for its oil, lavender is equally useful in a border for its dense stalks of dark purple flowers.

The parterres are planted with spike speedwell (*Veronica spicata*), a prostrate, mat-forming perennial native to Northern Europe, which sports a long-lasting, elongated blue flower. Each fall the parterres are underplanted with an assortment of spring-blooming bulbs including windflowers (*Anemone coronaria*), Dutch crocuses (*Crocus vernus*), and daffodils (*Narcissus Pseudonarcissus*). The circular bed with its upright tree box (*Buxus sempervirens 'Arborescens'*) is the focal point for the entire garden and, as such, is planted with a succession of colorful seasonal blooms. Surrounding the circle bed, for decoration, is a row of cockleshells, which are ancient, fossilized shells found in the marl banks along the James River near Carter's Grove.

The outside beds that flank this intimate garden are bordered with a hedge of common boxwoods clipped to a height of two feet. To the east, behind this low, formal hedge of box, roses bloom in season and are supplemented by the later flowering of single—and highly prized—hollyhocks (*Alcea rosea*) along the fence. The roses along the fence are old pink-blooming varieties of moss (*Rosa centifolia 'Muscosa'*) and damask (*Rosa damascena*) roses. The west side of the garden, alongside the Raleigh Tavern kitchen, is bounded by a row of common lilacs (*Syringa vulgaris*) that bloom in the late spring. The lilacs are unfortunately taxed by the temperate winters, hot summers, and high humidity of tidewater Virginia.

This long, narrow pleasure garden, which measures about thirty-five feet by ninety-five feet, is enclosed by a variety of different fences. Along the street is a highly decorative style of picket fence with one-inch-square pickets with carved points. These pickets are copied from an eighteenth-century design found in both England and Bermuda. A board fence with sawtooth pales separates this garden from the

(Above left) Early morning sunlight casts long shadows across the orchard. (Below left) A perennial border basks in the bright summer sun. (Above) White and pink garden phlox contrast nicely with the pale gray kitchen.

work yard at the Raleigh Tavern. Yet another style of picket fence, with sawn decorative tops in the shape of a spade, surrounds the work yard. The paths in the garden are paved with bricks in a flat running-bond pattern and are bordered with bricks set on edge.

Beyond the garden gate, flanked by a pair of boxwood topiaries and shaded by a picturesque sweet bay, lies the third component of this vista, the orchard. Perhaps the most exciting part of the Alexander Craig garden for the garden historian is the orchard planted in pears (*Pyrus communis*), peaches (*Prunus Persica*), and figs (*Ficus carica*). It is characteristically laid out in a series of square turf plots. The pattern for the orchard was established by the old brick paths. Though the paths were discovered, the use of the space was not. Rather than an orchard, this area may very well have been used as a kitchen garden, but it is difficult to know with certainty. In any case, the orchard serves the composition admirably.

The kitchen is directly behind the house, within its own work yard paved in a basket weave pattern of bricks. The walks have an interesting crazy-quilt pattern of brickbats. Brickbats are simply discarded pieces of bricks; in this case, they have been laid in a random pattern. A perennial border stretches along the west picket fence and features perennial phlox (*Phlox paniculata*), tawny daylilies (*Hemerocallis fulva*), wild columbines (*Aquilegia canadensis*), threadleaf tickseeds (*Coreopsis verticillata*), tickseeds (*Coreopsis lanceolata*), flag (*Iris X germanica*), New England asters (*Aster novae-angliae*), and black-eyed Susans (*Rudbeckia hirta*). Northeast of the house is a huge Carolina allspice (*Calycanthus floridus*), one of the largest shrubs of this type in Williamsburg.

The paddock, stable, and carriage house with access from the back street complete the layout of this lot.

(Above) A full crop of peaches.
(Below) Bright red single-flowered hollyhocks.

An orchard of crab apples.

dens for the pattern and style of the present garden. The parterre garden uses as its model a modification of the popular flag pattern repeating four crosses within the rectangular garden. The white oyster shell paths, the red brick edging, and the blue annuals that traditionally fill the parterre beds further elaborate the allusion to the red, white, and blue Great Union flag of Great Britain.

The garden is surrounded by a mature hedge of edging boxwoods (*Buxus sempervirens 'Suffruticosa'*) trimmed into loose mounds of about six feet in height. The north, or street, side of this hedge has been trimmed to the height of the picket fence to facilitate the view into the garden from the sidewalk. The parterres are edged with edging boxwoods clipped to a height of eighteen inches and are filled seasonally with white tulips (*Tulipa Gesnerana*) and Johnny-jump-ups (*Viola tricolor*) in the spring and blue and white rocket larkspurs (*Consolida ambigua*) in the summer.

At the rear of the lot lies the orchard with its own curious history. Visitors to the garden in the spring encounter masses of white-flowering crab apples (*Malus coronaria*) known locally as the Chiswell crab apple. These trees were propagated in the 1930s from a then existing ancient tree located at the Chiswell property on Francis Street. Subsequent investigations have led researchers to conclude that this is actually the Whitney crab apple that was popular in Virginia in the mid-nineteenth century. At the southern end of the property is a small Maupin family cemetery enclosed by a brick wall. The Maupin family owned the property in the middle of the nineteenth century.

The largest and most dominant shrub on the site is an old possum haw (*Ilex decidua*) at the southwest corner of the house, the largest possum haw in the Historic Area, and possibly the largest in the region. Possum haw, also known as swamp holly, is one of the deciduous hollies and will grow to twenty-five feet in height and width. The grayish twigs and branches are characteristic, and its berries, borne in small clusters, turn bright red-orange in the fall and remain on the tree until early spring, unless the birds discover them. Also of interest is the clipped hedge of American beeches (*Fagus grandifolia*) that encloses part of the orchard. The American beech is one of the most venerable trees of the southern forests, reaching heights of one hundred feet or more. In this case the hedge is trimmed to only eight feet, creating a dense and virtually impenetrable screen.

The pleasure garden's unique flag pattern.

CUSTIS TENEMENT

KEY TO THE PLAN
A. Custis Tenement
B. Kitchen
C. Privies
D. Wellhead
E. Kitchen Yard
F. Pleasure Garden
G. Orchard
H. Cemetery

PLANT LIST

TREES
1. Acer rubrum — Red maple
2. Acer saccharum — Sugar maple
3. Broussonetia papyrifera — Paper mulberry
4. Carpinus caroliniana — American hornbeam
5. Cercis canadensis — Redbud
6. Cornus florida — Flowering dogwood
7. Fagus grandifolia — American beech
8. Ficus carica — Common fig
9. Ilex decidua — Possum haw
10. Ilex opaca — American holly
11. Juniperus virginiana — Red cedar
12. Koelreuteria paniculata — Golden-rain tree
13. Lagerstroemia indica — Crape myrtle
14. Liquidambar Styraciflua — Sweet gum
15. Malus coronaria — Wild sweet crab apple
16. Quercus imbricaria — Shingle oak
17. Quercus nigra — Water oak

SHRUBS
18. Buxus sempervirens — Common boxwood
19. Buxus sempervirens 'Suffruticosa' — Edging boxwood
20. Calycanthus floridus — Carolina allspice
21. Myrica cerifera — Wax myrtle
22. Vitex Agnus-castus — Chaste tree

VINES
23. Campsis radicans — Trumpet creeper
24. Celastrus scandens — American bittersweet
25. Wisteria frutescens — American wisteria

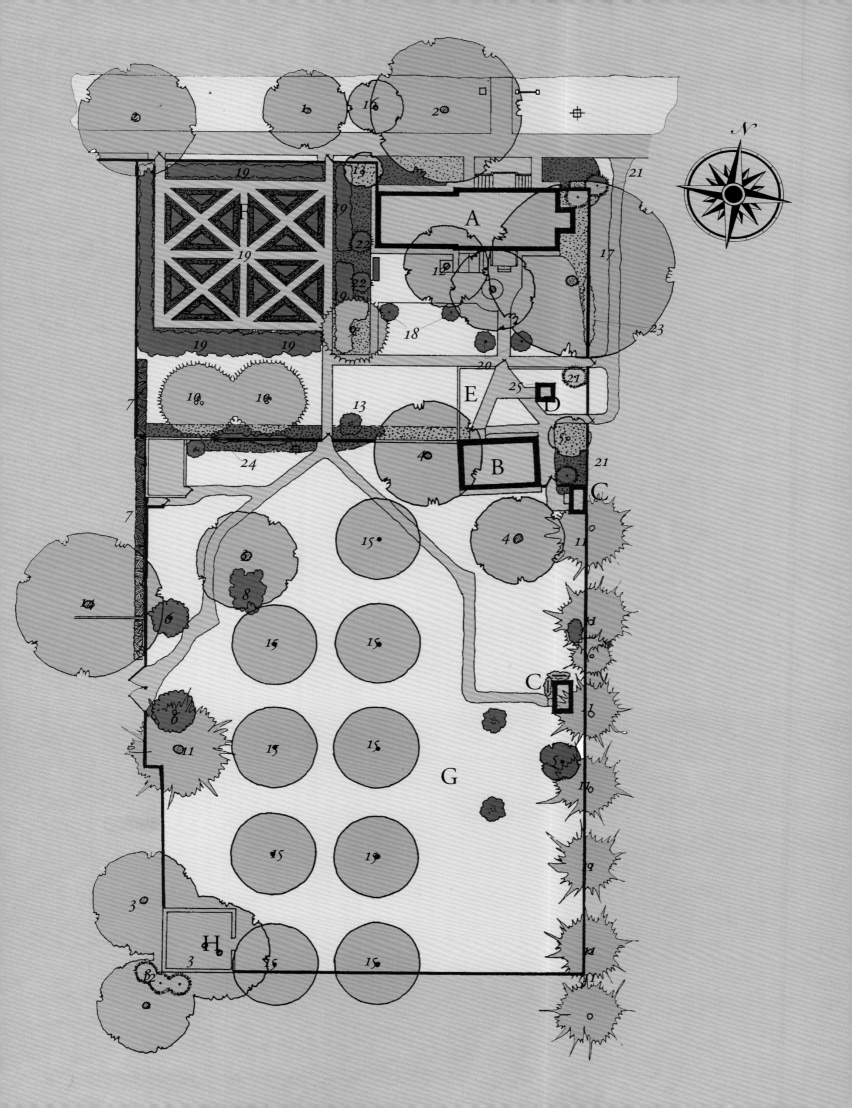

This pleasant reconstructed frame house, prominent on the Palace green, takes its name from a colorful Irish coachmaker by the name of Elkanah Deane. The first ownership of this property was recorded in 1720, when John Holloway was granted two lots facing Prince George Street. Holloway moved to Williamsburg in 1715 from King and Queen County and bought numerous lots in the city. In 1722, Holloway was named the first mayor of Williamsburg and later served as member and Speaker of the House of Burgesses and treasurer of the colony. He was the second husband of Elizabeth Cocke, sister of Mark Catesby, the acclaimed English naturalist.

In 1761, William Carter purchased the property, and by 1767 he had mortgaged the property to his brothers. A year later he advertised for sale "The Dwelling House in Palace street, with four Lots of Ground, well enclosed, and in good repair, where the subscriber now lives." Carter advertised the property for rent yet again in 1771.

About 1772, Elkanah Deane bought this property with its four lots of land, house, and outbuildings for seven hundred pounds and set up his business. Having met with coachmaking success in New York, where he obtained an order to make a coach, a phaeton, and a chaise for Governor Dunmore, Deane moved his family and business to Williamsburg. Business appears to have prospered for Deane, for on several occasions he advertised in the *Virginia Gazette* for apprentices. Described by one disgruntled rival in the *Virginia Gazette* as "an Hibernian Cottager" and the "Palace Street Puffer," Deane nonetheless earned a name for himself making and repairing all kinds of carriages.

Deane died in 1775 and his widow, Elizabeth, tried to sell the property by noting that there was "a well of good water on the lot . . . a fine garden and pasture at the back . . .

*Anemones herald the beginning of spring in the Elkanah
Deane garden. Oval, round, and rectangular beds are planted
in boxwoods and bulbs, annuals, and perennials. Small-leaved
European lindens provide a canopy overhead.*

all well paled in. . . . The houses [outbuildings] are in good repair, . . . some . . . but lately built." The property did not sell, so Elizabeth instead leased the shop to several tradesmen. Elizabeth Deane lived on the property until her death in 1784. By the turn of the century, records indicate that the buildings had disappeared.

THE ELKANAH DEANE GARDEN

A splendid formal garden under a planting of linden trees lies west of the house along Prince George Street. Since little archaeological evidence of a garden came to light, landscape architect Arthur A. Shurcliff's design of the pleasure garden is conjectural. It was adapted from patterns commonly used in southern gardens of the eighteenth century. This design is similar to one from Claude J. Sauthier's map of Edenton, North Carolina, drawn in 1769. The garden design is a sequence of spaces—oval, round, and rectangular parterres—planted in common boxwoods (*Buxus sempervirens*) and

filled with common periwinkles (*Vinca minor*) and spring bulbs. The progression of differently shaped parterres, an overhead canopy of small-leaved European lindens (*Tilia cordata*), and elaborate boxwood topiaries are the essential elements in this popular garden. Featured prominently in the garden, the lindens are small, slow-growing trees with heart-shaped dark green foliage with noticeably fragrant flowers. The long bed on the garden's north side contains bulbs, annuals, and perennials, providing abundant spring and summer color.

The topiary boxwoods that grace the parterres resemble interrupted cones, a form popular in English gardens of the seventeenth century. The topiaries in this garden are constructed from tree boxwood (*Buxus sempervirens 'Arborescens'*), or the upright form of common boxwood.

The Elkanah Deane garden is another of Colonial Williamsburg's gardens that has seen much change since it was designed and planted in the 1930s. Originally, the garden was richly decorated with many more topiary plants, extensive perennial borders, and massive bulb

(Above) The well as seen from the garden. (Left) A brightly colored clump of jonquils. (Right) A longitudinal view of the garden from the east gate.

displays. Continuing research in colonial gardening has revealed that it is unlikely that Elkanah Deane, a tradesman, would have had such an elegant garden. Thus the garden has been simplified over the years as it has matured. The massive canopy of mature lindens has made it increasingly difficult to maintain the long perennial borders, and their visual significance to the garden has diminished. Future archaeological investigations using the most modern techniques may answer the question of precisely what kind of garden the Deane family had here in the eighteenth century.

The east Deane privy is guarded by boxwood hedges and a layered topiary.

ELKANAH DEANE HOUSE

PLANT LIST

TREES

1.	Acer saccharum	Sugar maple
2.	Aesculus Pavia	Red buckeye
3.	Broussonetia papyrifera	Paper mulberry
4.	Carpinus caroliniana	American hornbeam
5.	Cercis canadensis	Redbud
6.	Fraxinus pennsylvanica	Green ash
7.	Ginkgo biloba	Maidenhair tree
8.	Juglans nigra	Black walnut
9.	Lagerstroemia indica	Crape myrtle
10.	Liquidambar Styraciflua	Sweet gum
11.	Maclura pomifera	Osage orange
12.	Malus pumila	Common apple
13.	Morus alba	White mulberry
14.	Platanus occidentalis	Eastern sycamore
15.	Prunus Cerasus	Sour cherry
16.	Prunus Persica	Peach
17.	Quercus alba	White oak
18.	Quercus rubra	Red oak
19.	Quercus velutina	Black oak
20.	Robinia Pseudoacacia	Black locust
21.	Tilia cordata	Small-leaved European linden
22.	Tsuga canadensis	Canada hemlock
23.	Ulmus alata	Winged elm
24.	Ulmus americana	American elm
25.	Ulmus procera	English elm

SHRUBS

26.	Buxus sempervirens	Common boxwood
27.	Ficus carica	Common fig
28.	Ilex vomitoria	Yaupon holly
29.	Myrica cerifera	Wax myrtle
30.	Ribes nigrum	European black currant
31.	Syringa vulgaris	Common lilac

VINES

32.	Campsis radicans	Trumpet creeper

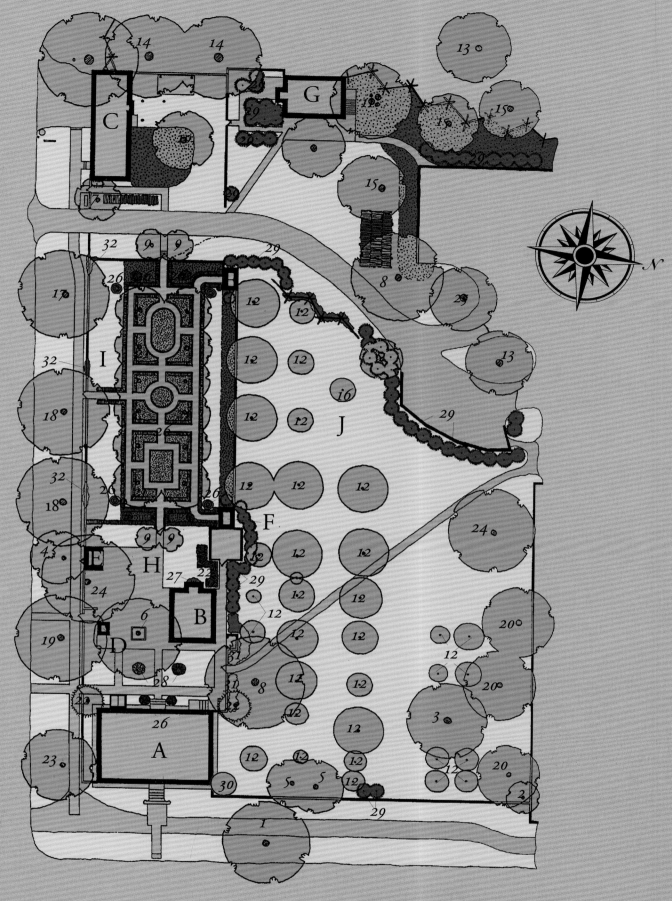

KEY TO THE PLAN

A. Elkanah Deane House
B. Kitchen
C. Harness Shop

D. Well
E. Woodshed
F. Privies

G. Servants' Quarters
H. Kitchen Yard
I. Pleasure Garden
J. Orchard

GOVERNOR'S PALACE

Dominating the north end of Palace green, the Governor's Palace was the symbol of the power and prestige of the British crown in colonial Virginia. This was the official residence of seven royal governors or lieutenant governors, from Alexander Spotswood, who supervised the construction of the building and the gardens, through Lord Dunmore, who fled from it in darkness one June morning in 1775. After the colony became a state, the Palace served as the executive mansion for Virginia's first two governors, Patrick Henry and Thomas Jefferson.

In 1706, after the new capitol building was completed in 1705, the General Assembly was prevailed upon to provide the necessary funding for the construction of a governor's mansion. Master builder Henry Cary, who had supervised the construction of the capitol, was placed in charge of this new project. Work

(Right) The ballroom garden with boxwood parterres and yaupon holly topiaries. Governor Alexander Spotswood supervised the construction of the gardens.

accelerated in 1710 with the arrival of Lieutenant Governor Alexander Spotswood, who devoted his personal attention to completing and expanding the project with the enclosure of the forecourt and the creation of elaborate gardens. Spotswood moved into the house in 1716, although work was to continue for several more years.

THE GOVERNOR'S PALACE GARDEN

As the building neared completion, the governor turned his attention to the gardens, greatly expanding them and laying out a series of terraces. The elaboration of the gardens and the spiraling costs that ensued reached such an extent that members of the Assembly began to express alarm at the expense. In disgust, Spotswood removed himself from any further involvement with the house and the grounds, writing that

Alexander Spotswood by Charles Bridges.

he would "surrender the Trust and Power, that I am by law possess'd of for Compleating the Governors House." From then on, all work at the Palace and its gardens was directed by the House of Burgesses, since it was built and maintained at the public's expense.

The complex of gardens with their manicured parterres and broad walkways provided pleasant distraction from the affairs of state. No doubt these impressive gardens served to enhance the prestige of the governor as the sole and legitimate representative of the crown and portrayed him as having the refinement and taste of his counterparts in England.

Precise layout and rigid symmetry were the bywords of English garden design in the early eighteenth century. Characteristic features at the Governor's Palace include elaborate geometrical parterres framed by clipped hedges and accented with topiaries, pleached beech allées offering shade and seclusion, and an intricate holly maze, a colonial variant of the contemporary English preoccupation with mazes.

In many respects the handsome and imposing layout of the house and grounds resembles English country estates during the reign of William and Mary. Dutch influence introduced into England by William III is discernible in both the house and the intricate ornamental gardens surrounding the mansion. Ultimately, the formal gardens and the orderly layout of the flanking buildings and outbuildings owe their origin to the Renaissance fascination with symmetry. Ironically, the Palace has come to symbolize the ultimate Virginia plantation house and spawned many imitators in the colonial—and modern—South.

(Right) The north garden with single late tulips.
(Below, left to right) The west side of the north garden.
The Palace across a sea of red tulips. Two views of diamond-shaped parterres of trimmed common boxwoods. (Overleaf)
The ballroom and north garden as seen across the fruit garden.

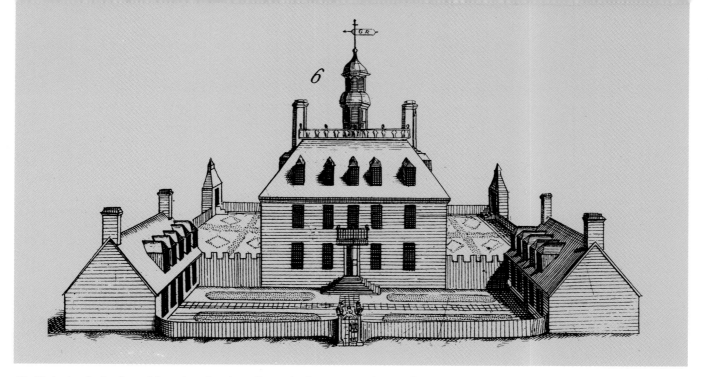

(Left) A pleached arbor of American beeches offers a shady retreat. (Above) The Governor's Palace. Detail from the Bodleian Plate.

THE FORECOURT GARDEN

The 1710 act that authorized completion of the Palace and building the gardens stipulated that a formal forecourt should grace the front of the Palace, and that a garden should be planted within that space. This area was to be level, enclosed by four-foot-high brick walls, and entered through handsome gates. This formal area has been reestablished and appears as it might have looked 250 years ago. As the Bodleian Plate suggests, the forecourt contains four oval parterres of clipped yaupon hollies (*Ilex vomitoria*), a red-berried native, surrounding panels planted with common periwinkles (*Vinca minor*). This highly formal garden space is a splendid complement to the symmetrical disposition of the flanking outbuildings and echoes the gravity and majesty of the mansion.

Prominent Plants

Ilex vomitoria	Yaupon holly
Maclura pomifera	Osage orange
Quercus phellos	Willow oak
Vinca minor	Common periwinkle

THE EAST SERVICE COURT

A complex of service buildings—the stables and carriage houses—at the east side served the transportation needs of the Palace. This service yard—and its counterpart on the west—was the center of daily life for many of the governor's household staff. Several fine old trees provide welcome shade for the service court.

Prominent Plants

Celtis occidentalis	Sugarberry
Ilex opaca	American holly
Quercus velutina	Black oak

THE HOLLY GARDEN

Just north of the East Flanking Building is a delightfully small garden whose inspiration came from the small courtyard gardens in Kips's engravings. Johannes Kips was a Dutch engraver and draftsman chiefly known for his extremely detailed illustrations of eighteenth-century English gardens. The center brick-edged parterres are planted with narrow borders of English ivy (*Hedera Helix*), seasonal bulbs, and annual flowers. Typically, the beds are filled with flowers in shades of yellow: yellow tulips (*Tulipa sp.*), English wallflowers (*Cheiranthus Cheiri*), yellow violas (*Viola cornuta*), pot marigolds (*Calendula officinalis*), and cowslips (*Primula veris*). In this shady setting the bright yellows add cheer in a garden dominated by hues of green.

Prominent Plants

Buxus sempervirens	Common boxwood
Hedera Helix	English ivy
Ilex opaca	American holly
Ilex vomitoria	Yaupon holly

THE BALLROOM
AND THE NORTH GARDEN

The gardens surrounding the Palace ballroom are representative of the formal design popular in the late

seventeenth-century gardens of English aristocrats who were themselves copying the latest royal style. There are no all-encompassing vistas here since this enclosed garden is intended to shut out the surrounding wilderness. With the exception of the ballroom addition added in 1752, this large garden appears as it might have during the tenure of Lieutenant Governor Alexander Spotswood. The garden is strictly geometric and symmetrical along the central north-south axis.

The upper, or ballroom, garden features eight diamond-shaped parterres and six cylindrical topiaries on each side of a central marl walk. Formed by short hedges of common boxwoods (*Buxus sempervirens*), the parterres are planted with English ivy (*Hedera Helix*) and common periwinkles (*Vinca minor*). The large yaupon holly (*Ilex vomitoria*) topiaries are actually several plants grown as one reaching almost the height of the ballroom itself. The topiaries are replicas of similar groupings seen on old English estates and often referred to as "the Twelve Apostles." The intricate patterning of this garden is meant to be seen and enjoyed from the windows of the upper floors or from the cupola of the Palace, where the viewer can "read" the garden's design from a higher and wider angle.

The north garden is equally symmetrical and formal. It features an allée of American beech trees (*Fagus grandifolia*) and large formal flower borders flanking the central axis. Running parallel with the flower borders at both the extreme east and west sides of the garden are a pair of pleached arbors, also of American beech. The garden is adorned with lead urns planted with Spanish-bayonet (*Yucca aloifolia*) on stone plinths.

In the spring thousands of brightly colored tulips fill the central flower beds, followed by annuals for the summer. The surrounding perennial borders feature many familiar flowers—daylilies (*Hemerocallis sp.*), perennial phlox (*Phlox paniculata*), and balloon flowers (*Platycodon grandiflorus*), among others.

Noteworthy are the pleached allées of American beech at the east and west side of the garden. The branches of the beeches interlace to form a tunnel without the help of additional support. Such tunnels, or galleries, as they are called, were a common feature of medieval English gardens. In the English climate they likely were planted for privacy; in the governor's garden they offer a shady path to the rear of the garden.

Prominent Plants

Buxus sempervirens	Common boxwood
Calycanthus floridus	Carolina allspice
Celastrus scandens	American bittersweet

(Above) The holly garden with four parterres planted with American hollies and English wallflowers. The central bed is planted in double-flowered late tulips. (Right) A typical feature in the English pleasure garden, the maze of American hollies offers a quiet diversion. (Overleaf) A swan glides serenely on Governor Spotswood's canal.

Danae racemosa	Alexandrian laurel
Decumaria barbara	Wood-vamp
Fagus grandifolia	American beech
Hedera Helix	English ivy
Hydrangea anomala petiolaris	Climbing hydrangea
Hydrangea quercifolia	Oakleaf hydrangea
Ilex vomitoria	Yaupon holly
Koelreuteria paniculata	Golden-rain tree
Lagerstroemia indica	Crape myrtle
Paeonia suffruticosa	Tree peony
Viburnum trilobum	Highbush cranberry
Vinca minor	Common periwinkle

THE MAZE AND MOUNT

The maze, loosely modeled after an ancient one still existing at Hampton Court in London, is undoubtedly the most popular attraction in Williamsburg's gardens. It is made of American hollies (*Ilex opaca*), a superb native plant for hedges. While there is no documented evidence that a maze existed here in the 1700s, records do indicate that there was a mount which served to insulate an icehouse in the ground beneath. Mounts were popular features of sixteenth-century English gardens, and in many instances the areas overlooked by mounts were planted as mazes. From the mount above, observers were entertained watching others find their way through the confusing maze. As a bonus, the Palace mount offers splendid views of the rest of the garden.

Prominent Plants

Ilex opaca	American holly
Rudbeckia hirta	Black-eyed Susan
Vinca major	Greater periwinkle
Vinca minor	Common periwinkle
Yucca filamentosa	Adam's-needle

THE FRUIT GARDEN

The fruit garden, with its cordoned apples and pears, espaliered plums, peaches, and figs, and large, round clairvoyée, or "window," is a sheltered location ideally suited to grow tender fruits. Cordons are fruit trees trained and pruned to grow along wires or other supports, in this case a frame of locust poles, whereas espaliers are fruit trees trained to grow in a flat plane against a wall, often in a geometric pattern.

In the southwest corner of the garden, foundations

The kitchen garden is filled with vegetables and herbs destined for the governor's table. (Overleaf) The kitchen garden's pear cordon in bloom.

for the steps of the nearby garden shed, and the north and west walls were revealed during archaeological excavations of the area. The Frenchman's Map indicated an L-shaped structure where the north and west walls are now located, which may have been an orangery or hothouse. Since the remains of this structure were not preserved well enough to determine its use or permit its reconstruction, the decision was made to enclose the space with a brick wall.

THE GRAVEYARD

South of the fruit garden lies a Revolutionary soldiers' graveyard. In the course of the garden excavations for the reconstruction of the Palace complex, a poignant story was revealed by the archaeologist's trowel. Investigators unearthed the graves of soldiers who had died from wounds while the Palace was serving as a military hospital during the Yorktown campaign. In eleven orderly rows, 156 unmarked graves were discovered, including those of two women thought to have been nurses. A simple stone tablet on a brick wall east of this space commemorates their sacrifice. Of note is the fact that the graves were arranged around what evidently were north-south and east-west pathways that once divided a garden into four squares. Today, edging boxwoods (*Buxus sempervirens 'Suffruticosa'*), shaded by laurel oaks (*Quercus laurifolia*), surround the turfed graveyard.

Prominent Plants

Buxus sempervirens	
'Suffruticosa'	Edging boxwood
Hedera Helix	English ivy
Quercus laurifolia	Laurel oak

THE BOXWOOD GARDEN

Arthur A. Shurcliff, who designed this garden, wrote, "The pattern of the garden, symmetrical on one axis, was derived in part from engravings of the ancient Physic Garden at Oxford, England, and in part from a garden in Edenton, North Carolina, measured by Sauthier in 1769." Annual flowers, bulbs, old roses, and a surrounding hedge of mature edging boxwoods add charm and considerable color to this secluded parterre garden. The garden's design is unusual in that it includes crape myrtles (*Lagerstroemia indica*) and American hollies (*Ilex opaca*) to provide shade as a concession to the heat of the Virginia sun. Classical parterre garden schemes would never have allowed trees to obscure the purity of the two-dimensional design.

Prominent Plants

Buxus sempervirens	
'Suffruticosa'	Edging boxwood
Ilex vomitoria	Yaupon holly
Ilex opaca	American holly
Quercus laurifolia	Laurel oak
Vinca minor	Common periwinkle

THE FALLING GARDENS AND CANAL

The falling gardens and canal date almost to the beginning of the Palace's history. In fact, the falling garden and "fish pond" were mentioned by a critical House of Burgesses as examples of "lavishing away" the colony's funds by Governor Alexander Spotswood. In his own defense, the governor later declared that he had discussed these gardens with "the Speaker and other Members" of the House when the gardens were under construction. Spotswood offered to fund the construction of these gardens himself if the colony was unwilling to pay for them.

The falling terraces, the long canal with overhanging trees, the quaint bridges, and the naturalistic plantings make the spot one of the most lyrical and bucolic in Williamsburg. This informal part of the garden is in marked contrast to the rigid geometry of the formal ballroom and north gardens.

Prominent Plants

Baccharis halimifolia	Groundsel tree
Betula nigra	River birch
Broussonetia papyrifera	Paper mulberry
Cephalanthus	
occidentalis	Buttonbush
Cornus florida	Flowering dogwood
Iris Pseudacorus	Yellow flag
Kalmia latifolia	Mountain laurel
Maclura pomifera	Osage orange
Myrica cerifera	Wax myrtle
Nyssa sylvatica	Black gum
Pinus Taeda	Loblolly pine
Tsuga canadensis	Canada hemlock
Ulmus americana	American elm

THE KITCHEN YARD AND VEGETABLE GARDEN

Beside the West Flanking Building is the service yard where the kitchen, scullery, laundry, smokehouse, and salthouse are located. Archaeologists found this important service area to be partially paved, just as visitors see

(Right) Spring bulbs carpet the boxwood garden.

it today. Trees provide shade to keep this work yard comfortable on hot summer days.

The kitchen garden, conveniently sited behind the kitchen, displays in season the many types of vegetables that graced the governor's table. Since this garden is too small to have provided all the produce necessary for the governor and his household staff, much was grown in outlying areas away from the kitchen proper. Additionally, fruits and vegetables were purchased in the town's market or brought in from farmlands set aside for the governor's use.

The terraced beds might have contained the culinary herbs and vegetables most commonly used by the cook, as they do today. The westward slope of the garden and the protection afforded by walls and fences makes a warm spot ideal for growing frost-sensitive fruits. Apricots (*Prunus Armeniaca*) are espaliered on the descending brick wall, and other fruits, including nectarines (*Prunus Persica var. nucipersica*), are grown against the wooden fence.

THE GOVERNOR'S PARK

The gardens, laid out much like those on early eighteenth-century English estates, served to frame pleasing views of distant views of pastoral scenery, or parks, planted with clumps of trees and shrubbery arranged informally for a picturesque effect. The governor's park is visible from the mount in the garden and can be seen through the delicate wrought-iron gates in the north garden. The governor's lands, which encompassed approximately 360 acres, have been reduced to about ten acres today. These lands would have included orchards, pastures, and gardens, and would have provided firewood and agricultural products. By virtue of his office, the governor also held title to 3,000 additional acres near Jamestown.

Governor Spotswood created two vistas from the Palace, the first, north across the park, and a second, south along the Palace green. Spotswood obtained permission from landowner John Custis to fell any trees that lay in the path of the vistas. However, the governor's men cut down two oaks that Custis had wanted for timber, thereby leading to a lasting disagreement between the two.

KEY TO THE PLAN

A.	Governor's Palace
B.	West Flanking Building
C.	East Flanking Building
D.	Coach House
E.	Stable
F.	State Coach House
G.	East Outbuilding
H.	East Outbuilding
I.	Rest Rooms
J.	Laundry
K.	Hexagonal
L.	West Well
M.	Salthouse
N.	Smokehouse
O.	Kitchen
P.	Scullery
Q.	Privy
R.	Tool House
S.	West Garden House
T.	East Garden House
AA.	Forecourt Garden
BB.	East Service Court
CC.	Kitchen Yard
DD.	Ballroom Garden
EE.	North Garden
FF.	Holly Garden
GG.	Bowling Green
HH.	Boxwood Garden
II.	Cemetery
JJ.	Fruit Garden
KK.	Vegetable and Herb Garden
LL.	Falling Gardens
MM.	Canal
NN.	Maze
OO.	Mount

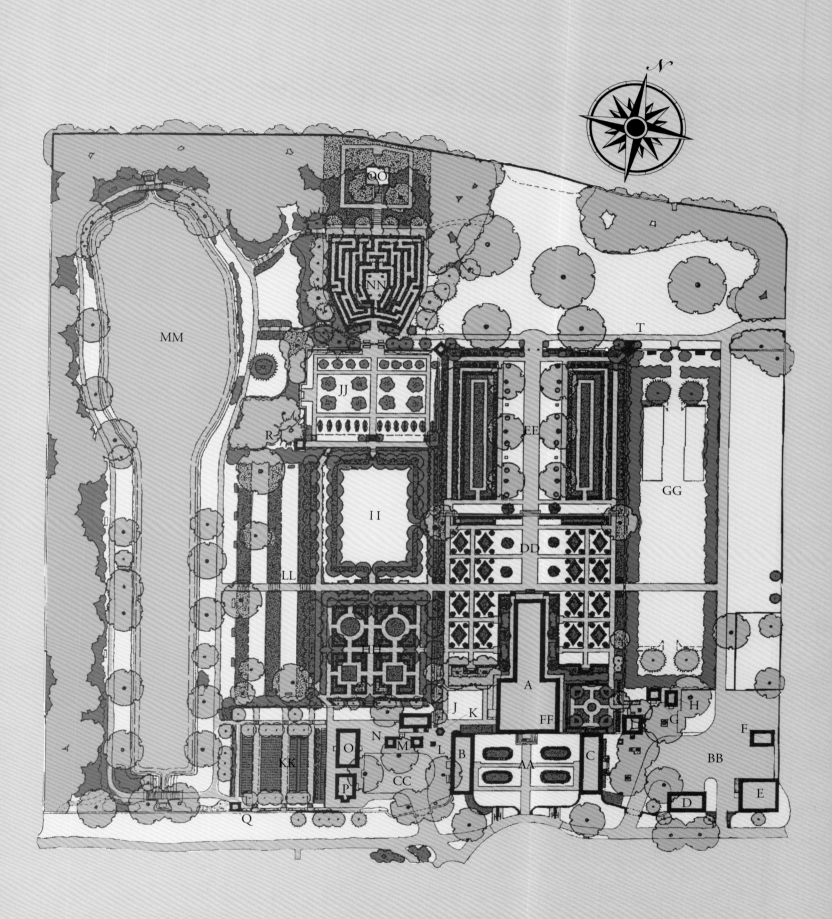

ORLANDO JONES HOUSE

This simple house with its distinctive projecting rear porch and compact oval garden is one of the most photographed in Colonial Williamsburg. The earliest known owner of this property was Orlando Jones, a planter and burgess, who purchased these two lots from the city trustees in 1716. He was the son of the Reverend Rowland Jones, the first rector of Bruton Parish Church. Jones married Martha Macon in January 1703, and their granddaughter, Martha Dandridge, married George Washington. Jones inherited from his father an extensive estate on Timson's Neck in York County. Since there was already a substantial brick house on it, Jones maintained his primary residence there. His Williamsburg property was probably a tenement.

A fire in 1842 swept away all of the houses that once stood on this block including the Orlando Jones House. Archaeological excavations on this lot in the 1930s revealed numerous brick foundations, as well as a brick drain running to the east, where a ravine existed in the eighteenth century. The modest size of the structure, its simple weatherboard construction, and the rear porch wing with a room above are typical of Virginia houses of the first quarter of the eighteenth century. The projecting porch chamber, one of only three examples in Williamsburg, was usually seen in late seventeenth-century buildings in Virginia like Bacon's Castle in Surry County.

THE ORLANDO JONES GARDEN

Since archaeological excavations revealed only scant evidence, the presence of a garden is based on the 1745 advertisement in the *Virginia Gazette* that indicates the existence of one at that time. Because of a ravine to the east (not filled until around 1780) the property during Jones's ownership was long and narrow. The Frenchman's Map helped to establish the location of fences on the site as seen today.

The garden was designed in 1939 by landscape architect Arthur A. Shurcliff and has remained almost unchanged since that time. Its design is atypical of eighteenth-century Virginia gardens which were usually of rectilinear geometry. This garden is an elongated oval set in a rectangular space defined by boxwood hedging and topiary shapes. Benches placed at each of the four corners provide a relaxing spot to read, study, or just enjoy the garden.

The garden features barrel-shaped topiaries of common boxwoods (*Buxus sempervirens*) on either side of the double privy and corkscrew-shaped boxwoods at the south end of the garden on both sides of the central axis. A kitchen garden was formerly located in the open area behind the privy in an area now in lawn for ease of maintenance.

There are several interesting features of this garden design. A large paper mulberry tree (*Broussonetia papyrifera*) placed off-center within the grassy oval

White lily-flowered tulips underplanted with English daisies highlight the oval pattern of the garden.

dominates the space and offers a counterpoint to the otherwise perfect regularity of the space. The flower beds, which follow the curve of the oval walk, are traditionally planted with white tulips for early spring color, reflecting the simplicity and understatement of the garden as a whole. Accent plantings of crape myrtles (*Lagerstroemia indica*) arch gracefully over the garden, lending their summer and fall color to the scene.

Visitors will enjoy spending a few moments sitting on the bench on the raised terrace at the south end of the garden. From this vantage point under the aerial hedge of American hornbeams (*Carpinus caroliniana*) is a lovely panoramic view of the garden with the house in the background. Aerial hedges, common in many European gardens, serve to define and frame space. In this setting, the hedge also provides a shady respite from the sun's heat on a summer day.

(Left) Tulips and English daisies. (Right) The complex of outbuildings adjacent to the garden. (Below) A garden bench is tucked into the rounded boxwood hedge.

(Above) Sheared boxwoods near the double privy.

ORLANDO JONES HOUSE

PLANT LIST

TREES

1.	Amelanchier canadensis	Shadbush
2.	Broussonetia papyrifera	Paper mulberry
3.	Carpinus caroliniana	American hornbeam
4.	Cornus florida	Flowering dogwood
5.	Diospyros virginiana	Common persimmon
6.	Halesia carolina	Wild olive
7.	Lagerstroemia indica	Crape myrtle
8.	Persea Borbonia	Red bay
9.	Quercus rubra	Red oak
10.	Quercus virginiana	Southern live oak
11.	Ulmus americana	American elm

SHRUBS

12.	Buxus sempervirens	Common boxwood
13.	Chaenomeles speciosa	Flowering quince
14.	Ilex vomitoria	Yaupon holly
15.	Myrica cerifera	Wax myrtle
16.	Osmanthus americanus	Devilwood

VINES

17.	Gelsemium sempervirens	Carolina jessamine
18.	Wisteria frutescens	American wisteria

(Above) Pink crape myrtles and the gnarled paper mulberry tree.

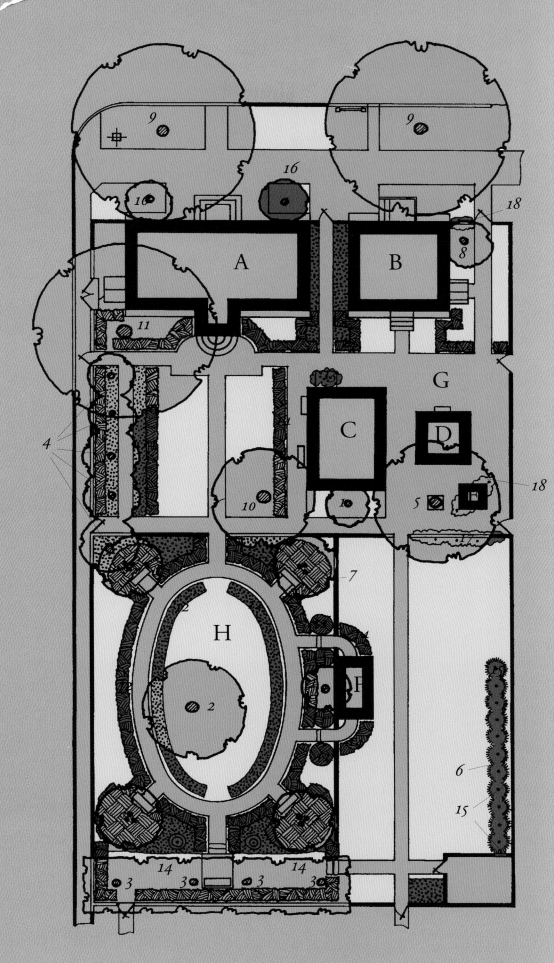

The site of one of the most prominent residences in eighteenth-century Williamsburg, the Lightfoot House and grounds command an expansive view of Market Square. Architectural evidence reveals that the house was originally constructed about 1730 as a two and one-half story double tenement and renovated in about 1750 for use as a town house. An eighteenth-century floor plan recently discovered among the papers of John Custis, the early Williamsburg botanist whose home was nearby on Francis Street, shows a four-family tenement closely resembling the type of rental property the Lightfoot House may once have been. Such tenements were reminiscent of speculative town houses commonly found in London.

It is believed that Colonel Philip Lightfoot, a wealthy Yorktown merchant and planter, owned the property early in the eighteenth century. While the earliest history of the Lightfoot property is unclear, research confirms parts of its later ownership. Philip Lightfoot III of Caroline County advertised the house for sale in 1783, describing it as "a large two-story brick dwelling house with four rooms on a floor . . . lying on the back street near to the market." William Lightfoot of Tedington inherited the house and other lots in Williamsburg and in 1786 sold them to the Reverend John Bracken, rector of Bruton Parish Church and subsequently president of the College of William and Mary.

The distinctive dusty red outbuildings—kitchen, laundry, smokehouse, dairy, and well—were reconstructed on original foundations discovered during the archaeological excavations in 1939 and again in 1949. The decorative fence across the front of the property shows the Chinese influence in colonial design, a style popular in both England and Virginia in the mid-eighteenth centu-

(Above) The simple formality of the garden echoes
the elegance of the Lightfoot House. (Left) An elaborate
wooden fence fronts the garden.

ry. The view of the garden glimpsed through the intricate design of the fence heightens the architectural distinction and stateliness of the Lightfoot House.

THE LIGHTFOOT GARDENS

The Lightfoot property, which in colonial days composed an entire block of eight lots, now encompasses only four of the original lots. Although reduced in size, the gardens, work yards, and small pastures give the complex an expansive, semirural feeling. The Frenchman's Map shows only two structures on this site, the main house and its kitchen, which are set apart at some distance from the street. The site, somewhat higher than Market Square, provides splendid views from one of the more prominent properties in the city.

Williamsburg's original building regulations required that structures along the town's main street be built a uniform six feet behind the front property line. Along the back streets, the setback was more discretionary; consequently, several dwellings on Francis Street are built further back. The Lightfoot House has the deepest setback, nearly seventy feet.

The formal space in front of the house is simple yet dignified. A central walk is flanked with sheared boxwoods (*Buxus sempervirens*), and mighty crape myrtles

(*Lagerstroemia indica*) in the four corners of the garden frame the quiet stateliness of the building. At the back of the house, the truncated property necessitated a shortened turf panel, terminated on the south by an effective screen of cherry laurels (*Prunus caroliniana*) and American hornbeam trees (*Carpinus caroliniana*). The rear garden is highlighted by purpleleaf myrobalan plums (*Prunus cerasifera*) and boxwoods set into a paisley pattern of English ivy (*Hedera Helix*). The beautifully espaliered southern magnolia (*Magnolia grandiflora*) against the west elevation of house is the finest example of this unique pruning technique in the city. A clipped yaupon holly hedge (*Ilex vomitoria*) flanks the garden and separates it from the kitchen yard to the east. A canopy of red oaks (*Quercus rubra*), red maples (*Acer rubrum*), pecans (*Carya illinoinensis*), loblolly pines (*Pinus taeda*), cherry laurels, and white mulberries (*Morus alba*) lends not only age and maturity to the site, but also a welcome respite from the sun.

The complex of service buildings with their yards and garden are east of the house. Facing the kitchen is

(Above) Native virgin's bower drapes along the garden fences.
(Right) Mixed single late- and lily-flowered tulips bloom over Johnny-jump-ups in the Lightfoot Tenement garden.

a brick-paved service yard, and a narrow brick path leads to the small laundry. Behind the kitchen is a small herb garden featuring intermingled herbs and flowers, tucked into a small nook separated from the pasture by a row of pomegranates (*Punica Granatum*) and a rustic picket fence.

THE LIGHTFOOT TENEMENT

This tenement on a corner lot next to South England Street was one of the seven adjoining properties that William Lightfoot sold to the Reverend John Bracken in 1786. Even though the term tenement meant a rented house, this building served at times as a store and a house. The Lightfoot Tenement, with a clipped gambrel roof, and its outbuildings have been reconstructed on their original foundations.

A much different garden has been designed for the Lightfoot Tenement than for the house. Garden beds are filled with seasonal annuals accented by boxwoods (*Buxus sempervirens*). An arching canopy of golden-rain trees (*Koelreuteria paniculata*) lends the garden abundant yellow summer color. A garden crosswalk leads from a pleached arbor of native redbuds (*Cercis canadensis*) to the well surrounded by clipped fruit trees. East of the tenement, an old gnarled smoke tree (*Cotinus Coggygria*) elicits comments from those unfamiliar with its puffy clouds of wispy white flowers that cover the tree like cotton. On the eastern fence line, virgin's bower (*Clematis virginiana*) adorns the board fence. Virgin's bower is a ubiquitous Virginia native vine that calls attention to itself in September with masses of sweetly scented white star-shaped flowers. Another distinctive plant found in this garden is the witch alder (*Fothergilla Gardenii*), a native shrub that sports white bottle brush flowers in April and turns a handsome orange-pink in autumn.

Two oblique views of the colorful Lightfoot Tenement garden.

Rarely blooming together, native redbud blankets the arbor and dogwood frames the view of the garden.

LIGHTFOOT HOUSE

PLANT LIST

TREES

1.	Acer rubrum	Red maple
2.	Alianthus altissima	Tree-of-heaven
3.	Broussonetia papyrifera	Paper mulberry
4.	Carpinus caroliniana	American hornbeam
5.	Carya illinoinensis	Pecan
6.	Cercis canadensis	Redbud
7.	Cornus florida	Flowering dogwood
8.	Cotinus Coggygria	Smoke tree
9.	Crataegus Phaenopyrum	Washington thorn
10.	Ilex opaca	American holly
11.	Ilex decidua	Possum haw
12.	Juglans nigra	Black walnut
13.	Juniperus virginiana	Red cedar
14.	Koelreuteria paniculata	Golden-rain tree
15.	Lagerstroemia indica	Crape myrtle
16.	Magnolia grandiflora	Southern magnolia
17.	Magnolia virginiana	Sweet bay
18.	Malus pumila	Common apple
19.	Morus rubra	Red mulberry
20.	Pinus Taeda	Loblolly pine
21.	Pinus virginiana	Scrub pine
22.	Prunus caroliniana	Cherry laurel
23.	Prunus cerasifera	Myrobalan plum
24.	Prunus domestica	Common plum
25.	Prunus Persica var. nucipersica	Nectarine
26.	Quercus palustris	Pin oak
27.	Robinia Pseudoacacia	Black locust
28.	Staphylea trifolia	American bladdernut
29.	Tilia americana	American linden

SHRUBS

30.	Buxus sempervirens 'Suffruticosa'	Edging boxwood
31.	Buxus sempervirens	Common boxwood
32.	Fothergilla Gardenii	Witch alder
33.	Ilex glabra	Inkberry
34.	Ilex vomitoria	Yaupon holly
35.	Illicium floridanum	Purple anise tree
36.	Myrica cerifera	Wax myrtle
37.	Punica Granatum	Pomegranate
38.	Taxus baccata	English yew

VINES

39.	Celastrus scandens	American bittersweet
40.	Clematis virginiana	Virgin's bower
41.	Gelsemium sempervirens	Carolina jessamine
42.	Wisteria sinensis	Chinese wisteria

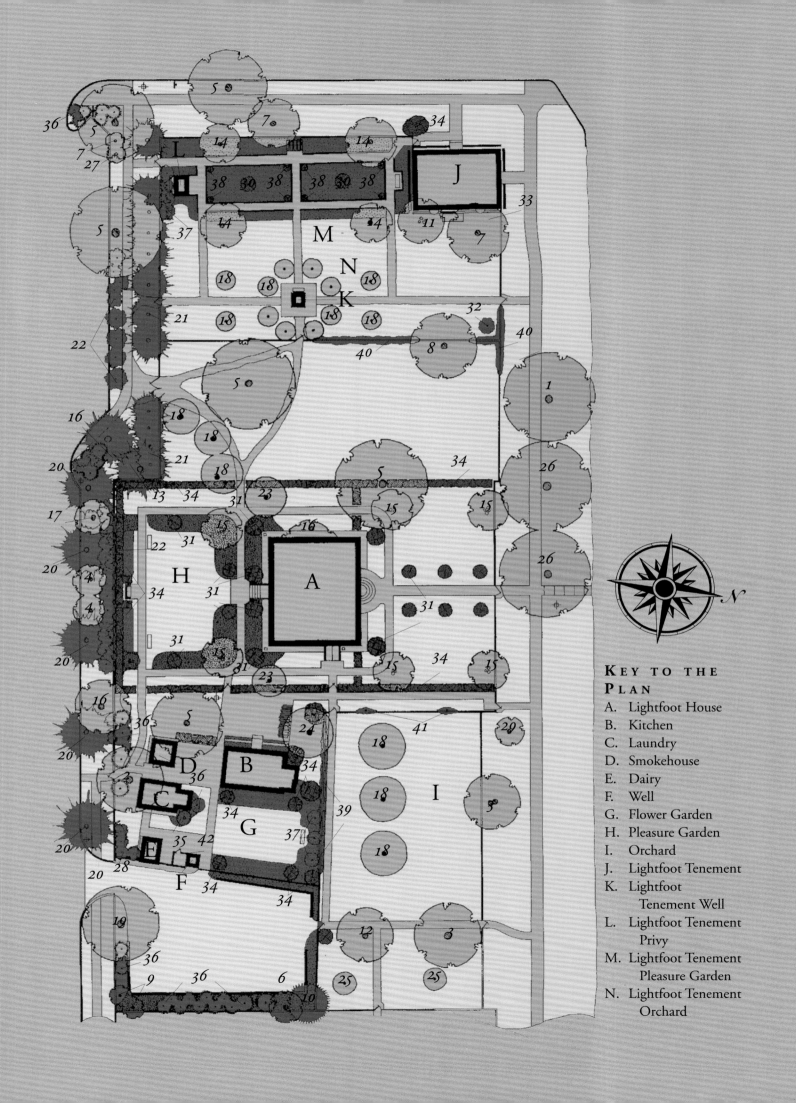

KEY TO THE
PLAN

A. Lightfoot House

B. Kitchen

C. Laundry

D. Smokehouse

E. Dairy

F. Well

G. Flower Garden

H. Pleasure Garden

I. Orchard

J. Lightfoot Tenement

K. Lightfoot
   Tenement Well

L. Lightfoot Tenement
   Privy

M. Lightfoot Tenement
   Pleasure Garden

N. Lightfoot Tenement
   Orchard

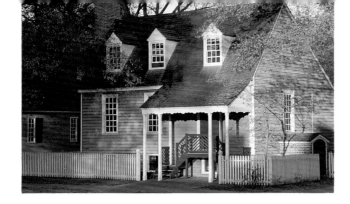

DAVID MORTON HOUSE

David Morton, a tailor, lived in this small one and one-half story house at the intersection of Waller and York Streets during the latter portion of the eighteenth century. Originally, the property was not in the city limits of Williamsburg but was annexed about 1750. Consequently, the lots at this end of town deviated from the more usual half-acre allotments prevalent within the original boundaries of the city. David Morton purchased the property from Benjamin Waller in 1777 for four hundred pounds, a sum that suggests the house and outbuildings were standing on the site at the time of sale.

The Frenchman's Map indicates the existence of three buildings on this corner that correspond to the Morton House, shop, and kitchen. The house seems to have been lived in continuously until it burned "sometime after the [Civil] War," as recalled Mr. John Charles, an elderly resident of Williamsburg writing in 1928. Mr. Charles described the house as a frame dwelling, facing Waller Street, with cellar steps on York Street. He also recalled it as a "house with [a] vine-clad porch."

Archaeological excavations in 1953 revealed the existence of foundations for the main house, which was a building thirty-two feet wide and thirty feet deep with a full cellar. Fragments of the foundations of the shop were found nearby, measuring ten by twenty-four feet, and complete foundations were uncovered for a kitchen, including its two large fireplaces. East of the house was a circular well lined with brick.

The formal garden is shaded by American hornbeam trees.

THE DAVID MORTON GARDEN

The position of the house and outbuildings, as shown on the Frenchman's Map and substantiated by archaeological excavations, was the determining factor in re-creating the garden. A paved service court provides convenient access between the house, shop, and kitchen. The surface treatment and the edging of the walks are typical of eighteenth-century examples found on nearby sites of comparable character.

The compact parterre garden on the east, or back, half of the lot is a treasure. Landscape architect Alden Hopkins adapted the basic design from a garden pattern

in the Charleston, South Carolina, plot books of 1787, specifically "Mr. Mey's Garden on Pinckney Street." The shape and effect of the boxwood-edged parterres are similar to those at the Bryan House at the west end of Duke of Gloucester Street.

The four rectangular parterres surround a covered well and pump, one of only two in Williamsburg—the other is at Market Square. Sour cherry trees (*Prunus Cerasus*) and lemon daylilies (*Hemerocallis Lilioasphodelus*) occupy the narrow beds that surround the parterre patterning. The boxwood (*Buxus sempervirens*) parterres are planted with common periwinkles (*Vinca minor*) and filled with Spanish bluebells (*Endymion hispanicus*), common grape hyacinths (*Muscari botryoides*), and white poet's narcissus (*Narcissus poeticus*) for spring color. The arbor, simple in character and constructed of hand-sawn lumber and skinned locust poles, terminates the garden along the north side of the lot with a shady retreat. A muscadine grape (*Vitis rotundifolia*) covers the arbor.

Between David Morton's tailor shop and the Isham Goddin lot next door is a small plum orchard (*Prunus domestica*) that helps screen the kitchen yard and its activities from the street. The walk from York Street to the same kitchen yard is lined with common figs (*Ficus carica*).

(Above) The symmetrical formal garden features boxwood parterres and a covered well and pump. (Left) Daffodils bloom in the Morton garden with the George Jackson House in the background.

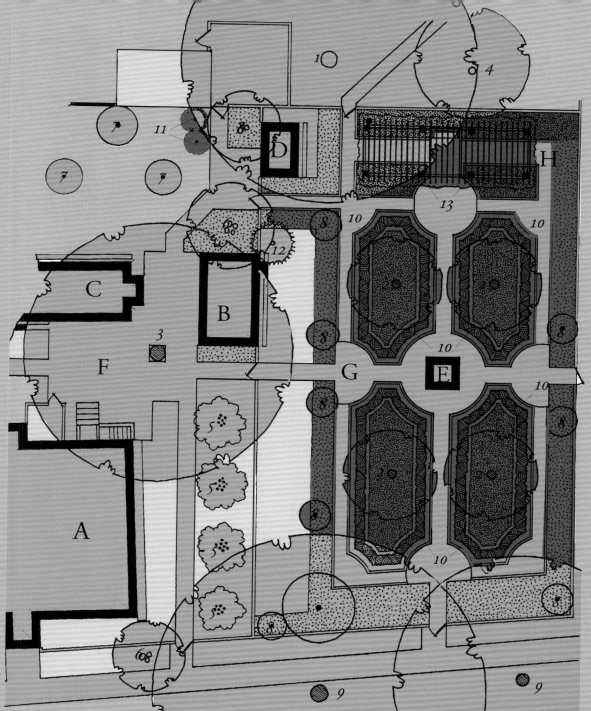

KEY TO THE PLAN
A. David Morton House
B. Kitchen
C. David Morton Shop
D. Privy
E. Well
F. Kitchen Yard
G. Formal Garden
H. Arbor

DAVID MORTON HOUSE

PLANT LIST

TREES

1. Acer rubrum — Red maple
2. Carpinus caroliniana — American hornbeam
3. Celtis occidentalis — Sugarberry
4. Cornus mas — Cornelian cherry
5. Ficus carica — Common fig
6. Lagerstroemia indica — Crape myrtle
7. Malus pumila — Common apple
8. Prunus Cerasus — Sour cherry
9. Quercus phellos — Willow oak

SHRUBS

10. Buxus sempervirens 'Suffruticosa' — Edging boxwood
11. Myrica cerifera — Wax myrtle
12. Vitex Agnus-castus — Chaste tree

VINES

13. Vitis rotundifolia — Muscadine grape

BENJAMIN POWELL HOUSE

The brick portion of this pleasantly idiosyncratic house with mismatched gables was built in the mid-eighteenth century by Benjamin Powell, a highly successful contractor responsible for building several of Williamsburg's public buildings. This lot, like the others on the east side of the Capitol, was carved out of a larger tract of property owned by Mann Page in 1747. It became the property of Benjamin Waller, who resold this lot to Benjamin Powell in 1763. He presumably built this house for his family's residence soon after.

A skilled carpenter, Benjamin Powell eventually became a successful Williamsburg building contractor. In 1769, he built the tower and steeple at Bruton Parish Church, and three years later he began construction on the newly authorized public hospital.

Powell sold the property in 1782. After changing hands several times, it became the property of Waller's grandson, Dr. Robert P. Waller, a physician. Dr. Waller's small brick office remains next to the house on the street.

An original eighteenth-century building, this dwelling,

shaped like the letter "L," went through at least two building periods. While the exact building chronology is unclear, the house has been restored to its appearance when the Powells lived there. The Powell kitchen, directly behind the main house, is another very old structure, dating from the 1830s. The building has a brick floor and two large fireplaces. The storehouse and stable are reconstructions on their eighteenth-century locations. The nineteenth-century office, smokehouse, and dairy are original.

THE BENJAMIN POWELL GARDEN
In the space between the house and the brick office lies a small square garden. Its brick paths are arranged like a four-spoke wagon wheel to outline pie-shaped beds edged in edging boxwoods (*Buxus sempervirens 'Suffruticosa'*) and seasonally filled with colorful annuals. The vertical scale of the garden is attained with flowering dogwoods (*Cornus florida*) and ancient crape myrtles (*Lagerstroemia indica*). Shoulder-high oakleaf hydrangeas (*Hydrangea quercifolia*) encircle the garden. In autumn, their reds echo the russets of the turning dogwoods and the oranges of the crape myrtles. Native ferns, peonies (*Paeonia lactiflora*), and mountain laurels (*Kalmia latifolia*) vie for space with the hydrangeas,

(Left) Brightly colored tulips fill the parterres in the Benjamin Powell garden. (Right) The Powell garden illustrates the axial arrangement of garden spaces typical of colonial site development.

while the fence across the front of the garden is festooned with native American wisterias (*Wisteria frutescens*).

Behind the pleasure garden and separated by a formidable hedge of common boxwoods (*Buxus sempervirens*) lies the work yard that connects the dairy, smokehouse, lumber house, kitchen, and well with the rear of the main house. This is the center of domestic activities for the family, and the space has the simple paving appropriate for a heavily used work space.

Beyond the outbuildings and the cross fence lies a kitchen garden featuring vegetables in season and a substantial herb plot located directly behind the smokehouse. Herbs, vegetables, and flowers were often interplanted for convenience as well as for an early version of what we today call "companion planting."

East of the kitchen garden lies a paddock; to the north is the stable yard with a reconstructed stable and henhouse. A small orchard north of the house is planted with apples (*Malus pumila*), peaches (*Prunus Persica*), sour cherries (*Prunus Cerasus*), and medlars (*Mespilus germanica*).

(Left) Interplanted onions and climbing beans maximize space in the vegetable garden. (Above) Dill shares space with single-flowered hollyhocks against the brick smokehouse. (Below) Cabbages, horseradishes, and onions are mainstays in the early spring kitchen garden.

BENJAMIN POWELL HOUSE

The brilliant fall foliage of crape myrtle and dogwood accentuates the reddish hues of the old brick dairy.

BENJAMIN POWELL HOUSE

PLANT LIST

TREES

1. Acer rubrum — Red maple
2. Aesculus Pavia — Red buckeye
3. Asimina triloba — Pawpaw
4. Carya illinoinensis — Pecan
5. Celtis occidentalis — Sugarberry
6. Cornus florida — Flowering dogwood
7. Ilex opaca — American holly
8. Lagerstroemia indica — Crape myrtle
9. Magnolia grandiflora — Southern magnolia
10. Malus pumila — Common apple
11. Mespilus germanica — Medlar
12. Prunus caroliniana — Cherry laurel
13. Prunus Cerasus — Sour cherry
14. Prunus Persica — Peach
15. Quercus alba — White oak
16. Ulmus americana — American elm

SHRUBS

17. Buxus sempervirens — Common boxwood
18. Buxus sempervirens 'Suffruticosa' — Edging boxwood
19. Chaenomeles speciosa — Flowering quince
20. Ficus carica — Common fig
21. Hydrangea quercifolia — Oakleaf hydrangea
22. Ilex vomitoria — Yaupon holly
23. Kalmia latifolia — Mountain laurel
24. Lonicera tatarica — Tatarian honeysuckle
25. Myrica cerifera — Wax myrtle
26. Philadelphus coronarius — Mock orange
27. Punica Granatum — Pomegranate
28. Rosa laevigata — Cherokee rose
29. Viburnum Tinus — Laurustinus

VINES

30. Campsis radicans — Trumpet creeper
31. Gelsemium sempervirens — Carolina jessamine
32. Vitis Labrusca — Fox grape
33. Wisteria frutescens — American wisteria

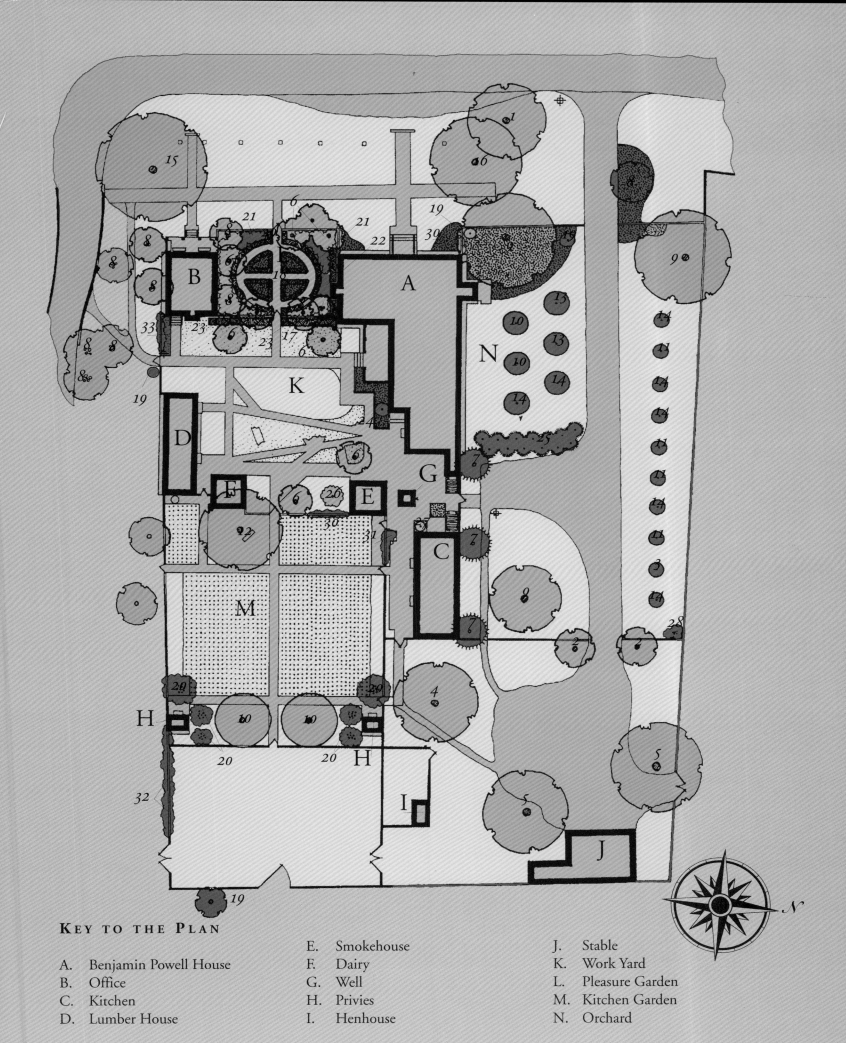

KEY TO THE PLAN

A. Benjamin Powell House

B. Office

C. Kitchen

D. Lumber House

E. Smokehouse

F. Dairy

G. Well

H. Privies

I. Henhouse

J. Stable

K. Work Yard

L. Pleasure Garden

M. Kitchen Garden

N. Orchard

PRENTIS HOUSE

The Prentis House at the northeast corner of Duke of Gloucester and Botetourt Streets was home to the family of a prosperous and influential Williamsburg merchant. Early York County records show that the property was purchased in 1712 by John Brooke from the Williamsburg city trustees. In 1725, he sold the house to his son-in-law, William Prentis. Although Prentis was the orphaned son of a London baker, research concludes that he received a thorough grounding in bookkeeping, accounting, and penmanship at Christ's Hospital in London before being apprenticed at age fifteen to Archibald Blair of Williamsburg. Prentis began his career as a bookkeeper and advanced to manager and later owner of "William Prentis and Company Merchants" in partnership with John Blair and Wilson Cary. His brick store building, built about 1740, still stands today on Duke of Gloucester Street just one block to the west of his house.

Before reconstruction, all the colonial buildings had disappeared completely, and a service station occupied the site. Archaeological excavations were particularly helpful in reconstructing this property, since the foundations for the house and several outbuildings were well preserved. The foundations for the house conformed to the sixty-four-foot length by thirty-one-foot depth noted in late

This overhead view of the garden features the Prentis House in the background. (Overleaf) An assortment of spring bulbs in the shade of a red buckeye tree.

eighteenth-century insurance policies. The construction of the foundation walls indicated that the main house went through three periods of enlargement.

THE PRENTIS GARDEN

Visually alive with the colors of hundreds of bulbs in the spring, this garden is one of Williamsburg's best garden shows. The property is an excellent example of garden development to the fullest degree within the confines of a typical one-half-acre lot. From Botetourt Street there is a good view of the succession of outbuildings: the flanking storehouse and kitchen, a dairy, a smokehouse, and a wellhead cluster around a paved yard, with a stable at the back of the lot. A central walk lines up with the back door, skirts around the wellhead, and divides the formal garden into two halves. Several cherished old red cedars (*Juniperus virginiana*) dominate the back of the property.

The formal pleasure garden lies within one of the enclosures behind the service yard. The space has been designed with six similar parterres edged in yaupon hollies (*Ilex vomitoria*). The squares at each end are

accented with red buckeye trees (*Aesculus Pavia*) underplanted with common periwinkles (*Vinca minor*) and spring bulbs; the center squares are in lawn. The distinctive hedges are trimmed with elaborate curved corners. The parterres are bordered with a board set on edge, a common edging in eighteenth-century gardening. Flanking the parterres are flower beds traditionally planted with tulips (*Tulipa sp.*) followed with colorful flowers in the summer. A line of pomegranates (*Punica Granatum*) screens the garden from Nicholson Street.

Laid out in simple squares, the kitchen garden parallels the formal garden on the east side of the lot. A small orchard near the back street is balanced by the stable and paddock at the rear of the site.

A family diary and garden planting lists proved to be quite valuable in re-creating the garden. Designed in the late 1930s by Arthur A. Shurcliff, only minor modifications have been necessary through the years. For example, the parterres were originally planted in roses, but they were later changed to shadbushes (*Amelanchier canadensis*) for additional shade. As the shadbushes matured and died, they were replaced with today's red buckeyes.

(Above and left) The privy dominates the northwest corner of the Prentis House garden. (Right) The well supports an American wisteria vine.

Snow blankets the Prentis garden

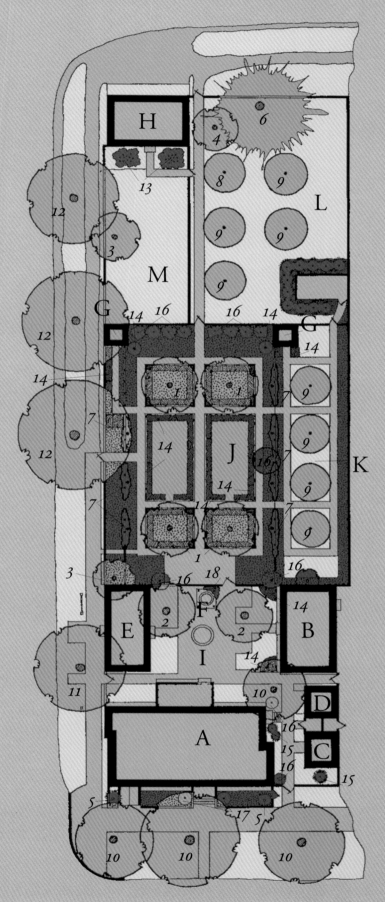

PRENTIS HOUSE

KEY TO THE PLAN
A. Prentis House
B. Kitchen
C. Smokehouse
D. Dairy
E. Shop
F. Well
G. Privy
H. Stable
I. Kitchen Yard
J. Pleasure Garden
K. Flower/Herb Garden
L. Orchard
M. Paddock

PLANT LIST

TREES
1.	Aesculus Pavia	Red buckeye
2.	Broussonetia papyrifera	Paper mulberry
3.	Cercis canadensis	Redbud
4.	Cornus florida	Flowering dogwood
5.	Ilex opaca	American holly
6.	Juniperus virginiana	Red cedar
7.	Malus pumila	Common apple
8.	Prunus Cerasus	Sour cherry
9.	Prunus Persica	Peach
10.	Quercus falcata	Spanish red oak
11.	Quercus phellos	Willow oak
12.	Quercus virginiana	Southern live oak

SHRUBS
13.	Ficus carica	Common fig
14.	Ilex vomitoria	Yaupon holly
15.	Myrica cerifera	Wax myrtle
16.	Punica Granatum	Pomegranate
17.	Viburnum tinus	Laurustinus

VINES
18.	Wisteria frutescens	American wisteria

(Above left) Globe amaranths. (Below left) Garden phlox.

SHIELDS TAVERN

ne of several licensed taverns in Williamsburg, Shields catered to the middling and well-to-do ranks of local residents and visitors. The reconstructed tavern depicts the era of about 1750 when James Shields lived there with his family and kept a tavern.

John Marot, a Huguenot refugee, received a license to operate a tavern in Williamsburg and in 1708 purchased this property on Duke of Gloucester Street where a building already stood. The existing building was only a small house, so Marot built an addition that more than doubled the size of the tavern. About 1738, James Shields married one of Marot's daughters and took over operation of the tavern. By 1750, Shields was dead, and soon after his widow married Henry Wetherburn, the proprietor of Wetherburn's Tavern. After 1752, the building was no longer used as a tavern. It later became a store, a residence, and, in time, a rental property.

Reconstruction of the tavern and the six outbuildings was based on a combination of documentary and archaeological evidence. A 1770 lease of the property indicates that the former tavern was divided into two tenements. The larger building was destroyed by fire in 1858, but the fate of the other building is not known.

A simple picket fence separates the kitchen garden from Shields Tavern.

THE SHIELDS TAVERN GARDEN

The garden in the rear yard began to come to light when further archaeological excavations were conducted by Colonial Williamsburg due to the building's conversion to an operating tavern in 1989. These investigations revealed the layout of the site: fence lines, walkways, wells, garden beds, and the pattern of the outbuildings.

The area directly behind the tavern is an outdoor dining area. To accommodate the needs of patrons, plantings are confined to the periphery, where they soften the white picket fences that surround the area. Planting beds filled with lemon daylilies (*Hemerocallis Lilioasphodelus*), Siberian iris (*Iris sibirica*), common periwinkles (*Vinca minor*), hollyhocks (*Alcea rosea*), tickseed (*Coreopsis lanceolata*), and informal seasonal bulbs add understated color throughout the year.

The large kitchen garden is laid out on the site of eighteenth-century planting beds. Similar in appearance to the vegetable garden at Wetherburn's Tavern, the overall visual effect is deliberately loose, even haphazard. Most of the space is given over to the cultivation of food crops—peas, beans, lettuce, cabbages, squash, onions, celery, parsnips, beets, radishes, salsify, collards, and mustard greens. The fruit trees include figs (*Ficus carica*) and greengage plums (*Prunus domestica* 'Greengage') at the rear gate.

Lemon-yellow daylilies, here blooming at the tavern, bloom later in the season than the more common orange-flowered, tawny daylilies.

PLANT LIST

TREES

1.	Acer saccharum	Sugar maple
2.	Carya illinoinensis	Pecan
3.	Chionanthus virginicus	Old-man's-beard
4.	Crataegus Phaenopyrum	Washington thorn
5.	Fraxinus americana	White ash
6.	Koelreuteria paniculata	Golden-rain tree
7.	Lagerstroemia indica	Crape myrtle
8.	Liriodendron Tulipifera	Tulip poplar
9.	Platanus occidentalis	Eastern sycamore
10.	Prunus domestica 'Greengage'	Greengage plum
11.	Ulmus rubra	Slippery elm
12.	Quercus alba	White oak

SHRUBS

13.	Buxus sempervirens	Common boxwood
14.	Calycanthus floridus	Carolina allspice
15.	Chaenomeles speciosa	Flowering quince
16.	Ficus carica	Common fig
17.	Hibiscus syriacus	Rose-of-Sharon
18.	Hydrangea quercifolia	Oakleaf hydrangea
19.	Ilex vomitoria	Yaupon holly
20.	Myrica cerifera	Wax myrtle
21.	Philadelphus coronarius	Mock orange
22.	Prunus caroliniana	Cherry laurel
23.	Punica Granatum	Pomegranate
24.	Vitex Agnus-castus	Chaste tree
25.	Vitex Negundo var. 'heterophylla'	Cutleaf chaste tree
26.	Yucca filamentosa	Adam's-needle

VINES

27.	Campsis radicans	Trumpet creeper
28.	Gelsemium sempervirens	Carolina jessamine
29.	Rosa laevigata	Cherokee rose

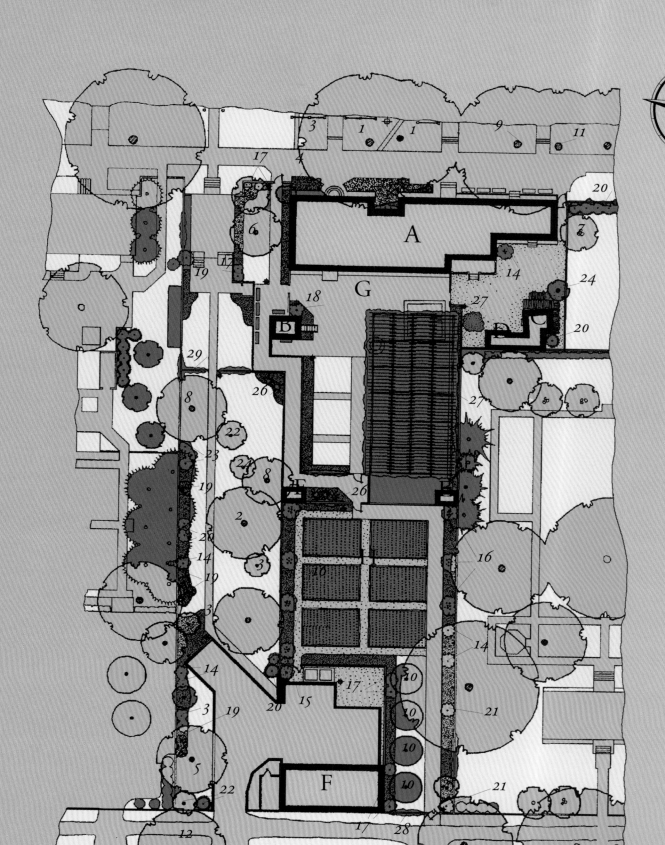

TALIAFERRO-COLE HOUSE

This lot at the corner of Nassau and Duke of Gloucester Streets has an interesting association with one of eighteenth-century Williamsburg's few professional gardeners, Thomas Crease. The first recorded ownership of this property dates to 1724, when Crease and his wife, Mary, were mentioned as living on the half-acre lot. Although little is known of Crease's early life, he was probably born in England and trained as a professional gardener before emigrating to the Virginia colony.

Thomas Crease may well have been the same gardener who worked occasionally for William Byrd II of Westover, whom Byrd called "Tom Cross" in a 1720 reference. He may have also worked for Byrd's brother-in-law, John Custis, as it is known that "Cross" brought Byrd a letter from Custis during one of his Westover visits. The possibility that Crease and "Cross" were the same is reinforced by the fact that Custis was an accomplished plantsman, with one of the finest gardens in the colonies, and likely relied on the talents of a competent, professional gardener. Crease lived within sight of Custis's property across Francis Street, and that they knew each other and shared their gardening interests seems beyond doubt.

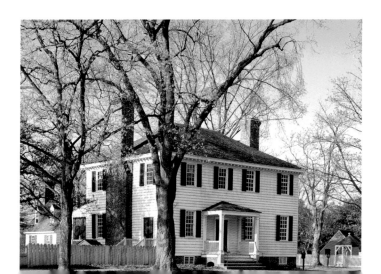

A mid-spring view of the pleasure garden, which features bulbs and perennials.

Thomas Crease is one of two gardeners in eighteenth-century Williamsburg known to have worked at both the Palace and the college. He worked as head gardener at the Governor's Palace during the administrations of Alexander Spotswood, who served from 1710 to 1722, and Hugh Drysdale, who served from 1722 until 1726. Crease then worked at the college until his death in 1756. A *Virginia Gazette* advertisement he placed on January 13, 1737, tells a great deal about this man: "GENTLEMEN and others, may be supply'd with good Garden Pease, Beans and several other Sorts of Garden Seeds. Also, with great Choice of Flower Roots; likewise Trees of several Sorts and Sizes, fit to plant, as Ornaments in Gentlemen's Gardens, at very reasonable Rates, by Thomas Crease, Gardener to the College, in Williamsburg."

Following the death of Crease, there is a gap in the chain of ownership of this property until 1773, when Charles Taliaferro (pronounced "Toliver") and his family occupied the house. Taliaferro was a well known and respected chairmaker and coachmaker who had been

plying his trade in Williamsburg since 1761. After his death, the property was sold to the Cole family in 1804, where it remained until purchased by Colonial Williamsburg in 1939.

THE TALIAFERRO-COLE GARDEN
Crease lived on this site for a total of thirty-three years, and it is likely that he maintained his own fine garden here. Dropping ten feet from the street to a ravine toward the rear, and offering a natural variation of levels, different exposures, and soil conditions and a ready water supply, this site would appeal to any gardener. The topography of the site is largely unchanged from its eighteenth-century character. The location of fences dividing the property was determined by the Frenchman's Map and colonial Virginia precedents. Some of the walks in the garden and on the lower terrace were revealed by archaeological excavations.

(Above) An aerial view of the terraced site. (Right) Early morning sunlight casts long shadows over the flower garden.

These gardens, designed by landscape architect Arthur A. Shurcliff, consist of three separate rectangular areas enclosed by fencing, each planted for a different purpose. The flower garden is laid out with a central turf panel and planting beds bordering the walks. This garden contains horticultural interest in every season of the year. A colorful array of spring bulbs, summer perennials, flowering trees, and shrubs makes the Taliaferro-Cole garden one of the most delightful in Williamsburg.

Many visitors notice with interest the "pollarded" eastern sycamore (*Platanus occidentalis*) trees planted at the rear of the property. The knotty appearance of these trees results from a pruning technique which involves the hard pruning of the previous season's growth back to the same knots or boles that are evident at the ends of branches. They are, in fact, accumulations of scar tissue that develop after many years of annual pruning. While this practice gives the sycamores an unusual appearance, it is not detrimental to their health. Infrequently seen in American gardens, pollarded trees and shrubs are common in European landscapes.

(Right) Single late tulips and a unique picket fence in the garden. (Below) Unusual pollarded eastern sycamore trees near the coach house.

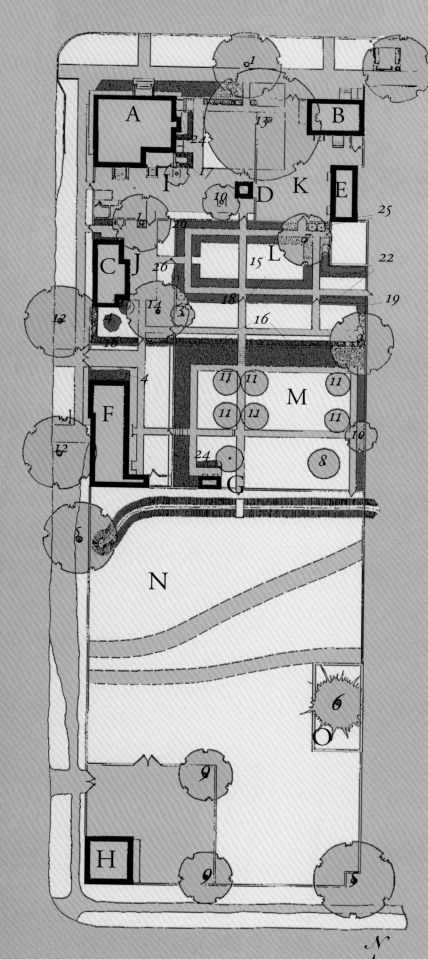

TALIAFERRO-COLE HOUSE

KEY TO THE PLAN

A. Taliaferro-Cole House
B. Shop
C. Kitchen
D. Smokehouse
E. Laundry
F. Stable
G. Privy
H. Coach House

I. House Yard
J. Kitchen Yard
K. Shop Yard
L. Pleasure Garden
M. Orchard
N. Paddock
O. Cemetery

PLANT LIST

TREES

1.	Acer saccharum	Sugar maple
2.	Broussonetia papyrifera	Paper mulberry
3.	Cornus florida	Flowering dogwood
4.	Ficus carica	Common fig
5.	Juglans nigra	Black walnut
6.	Juniperus virginiana	Red cedar
7.	Lagerstroemia indica	Crape myrtle
8.	Malus pumila	Common apple
9.	Platanus occidentalis	Eastern sycamore
10.	Prunus cerasifera	Myrobalan plum
11.	Prunus Persica	Peach
12.	Quercus phellos	Willow oak
13.	Quercus virginiana	Southern live oak
14.	Tilia cordata	Small-leaved European linden

SHRUBS

15.	Aronia arbutifolia	Red chokeberry
16.	Buxus sempervirens	Common boxwood
17.	Buxus sempervirens 'Suffruticosa'	Edging boxwood
18.	Clethra alnifolia	Summer-sweet
19.	Cornus Amomum	Silky dogwood
20.	Ilex verticillata	Winterberry
21.	Philadelphus coronarius	Mock orange
22.	Spiraea tomentosa	Hardhack
23.	Symphoricarpos orbiculatus	Indian currant
24.	Syringa vulgaris	Common lilac
25.	Viburnum dentatum	Southern arrowwood

VINES

26.	Wisteria frutescens	American wisteria

(Left) Colorful spring-flowering larkspurs dominate this view of the Taliaferro-Cole Kitchen.

BENJAMIN WALLER HOUSE

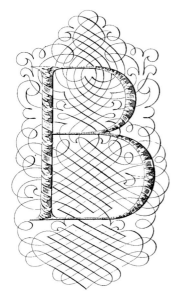

Benjamin Waller, a respected and influential lawyer and community leader, purchased this property before 1750. When he died in 1786, it was a sprawling complex with an elegant garden. Waller was the youngest member of a large and distinguished King William County family. Waller probably attended the grammar school at William and Mary in the late 1720s and then apprenticed in the office of the secretary of the colony, John Carter. During an impressive career, Waller held a variety of offices, serving as burgess, city recorder, judge of the Court of Admiralty, and vestryman of Bruton Parish Church. He practiced law and was a tutor to George Wythe, who became one of the most influential lawyers, teachers, and legal philosophers of his time. When Waller died, the house and garden passed to William Waller, his grandson, and his wife, Elizabeth, the daughter of President John Tyler. The property remained in family hands for well over one hundred years.

The Waller House is another of the surviving original colonial-era buildings in Williamsburg, and like many other old dwellings, this house is the product of several building phases. With the exception of an original smokehouse, the outbuildings are reconstructions. They include the dairy, henhouse, storehouse, garden house, well, kitchen, stable, office, and the privies. A number of walks and paved areas were discovered during the archaeological excavations in 1950. The circular pavement at the kitchen door is a faithful reproduction of the original pattern, and the many unearthed marl walks contributed to the faithful re-creation of the formal garden and house yard.

In the front yard a small office stands at a right angle to the main house, facing west along Francis Street. This building, which appeared on the Frenchman's Map and was verified by archaeology, was Benjamin Waller's law office.

THE BENJAMIN WALLER GARDEN

Sketches of Williamsburg lot layouts have survived through deeds and insurance documents; however, surviving actual garden layouts are almost nonexistent. In the case of the Waller garden, the discovery of a crude drawing of the garden among the papers of Miss Luty Blow led to the restoration of the garden. Miss Blow's grandmother was Eliza Waller, a granddaughter of Benjamin Waller. She was so fond of her grandfather's Williamsburg garden that she built a replica at Tower Hill, her home in Surry County. In the early twentieth century, Luty drew a sketch of that garden from mem-

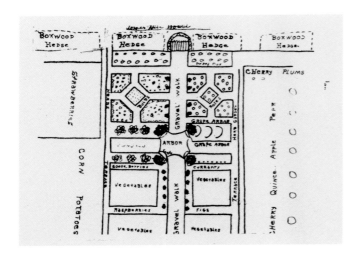

(Left) Luty Blow's sketch of her ancestor's garden.
(Right) The re-created garden today with the Benjamin Waller House in the background. (Overleaf) Boxwood parterres, unique fence pickets, and the garden house.

ory. This drawing, along with the archaeological evidence, resulted in one of the best-documented gardens in Williamsburg.

Although traces of the garden had disappeared except for the central walk built of marl and gravel, the garden in Luty Blow's sketch fit perfectly within the area between the graveyard at the rear of the lot and the house. Although the planting pattern was not followed exactly, the long north-south central walk leads from the house to the graveyard and bisects the formal garden. The arbor shown at the intersection of the walks was replaced with a small pavilion set within the formal beds. Edging boxwoods (*Buxus sempervirens 'Suffruticosa'*) edge the beds filled with common periwinkles (*Vinca minor*) and accented with gold-dust tree (*Aucuba*

japonica Variegata) shrubs. Surrounding borders are planted with edging and common boxwoods (*Buxus sempervirens*) and pomegranates (*Punica Granatum*). Cherokee roses (*Rosa laevigata*) grow against the garden house and small-leaved European lindens (*Tilia cordata*) provide shade. Spring and summer bulbs highlight this garden in their seasons.

Restoration of the property as a whole was aided by the survival of the eighteenth-century marl walks. Fence lines, determined partly by postholes and partly by the location of the outbuildings, gave researchers a feel for how the property was organized. Reproduction of the fence pickets was made possible by the discovery of a surviving picket used in construction of the dormers on the house.

The comprehensive nature of the Waller site with its full complement of outbuildings, substantial garden, and original house makes this one of the most complete and compelling settings in Williamsburg.

A late summer view of the garden house and the garden with the spider lilies in bloom.

BENJAMIN WALLER HOUSE

PLANT LIST

TREES

1.	Acer saccharum	Sugar maple
2.	Broussonetia papyrifera	Paper mulberry
3.	Carya illinoinensis	Pecan
4.	Celtis occidentalis	Sugarberry
5.	Cercis canadensis	Redbud
6.	Cornus florida	Flowering dogwood
7.	Diospyros virginiana	Common persimmon
8.	Juglans nigra	Black walnut
9.	Juniperus virginiana	Red cedar
10.	Lagerstroemia indica	Crape myrtle
11.	Magnolia grandiflora	Southern magnolia
12.	Malus pumila	Common apple
13.	Morus alba	White mulberry
14.	Picea Abies	Norway spruce
15.	Pinus Taeda	Loblolly pine
16.	Pinus Strobus	Eastern white pine
17.	Platanus occidentalis	Eastern sycamore
18.	Robinia Pseudoacacia	Black locust
19.	Tilia cordata	Small-leaved European linden
20.	Ulmus americana	American elm

SHRUBS

21.	Aucuba japonica Variegata	Gold-dust tree
22.	Buxus sempervirens	Common boxwood
23.	Buxus sempervirens 'Suffruticosa'	Edging boxwood
24.	Calycanthus floridus	Carolina allspice
25.	Chaenomeles speciosa	Flowering quince
26.	Ficus carica	Common fig
27.	Hibiscus syriacus	Rose-of-Sharon
28.	Hydrangea quercifolia	Oakleaf hydrangea
29.	Ilex vomitoria	Yaupon holly
30.	Myrica cerifera	Wax myrtle
31.	Philadelphus coronarius	Mock orange
32.	Punica Granatum	Pomegranate
33.	Rhus aromatica	Fragrant sumac
34.	Rosa Roxburghii	Chestnut rose
35.	Vitex Agnus-castus	Chaste tree
36.	Yucca filamentosa	Adam's-needle

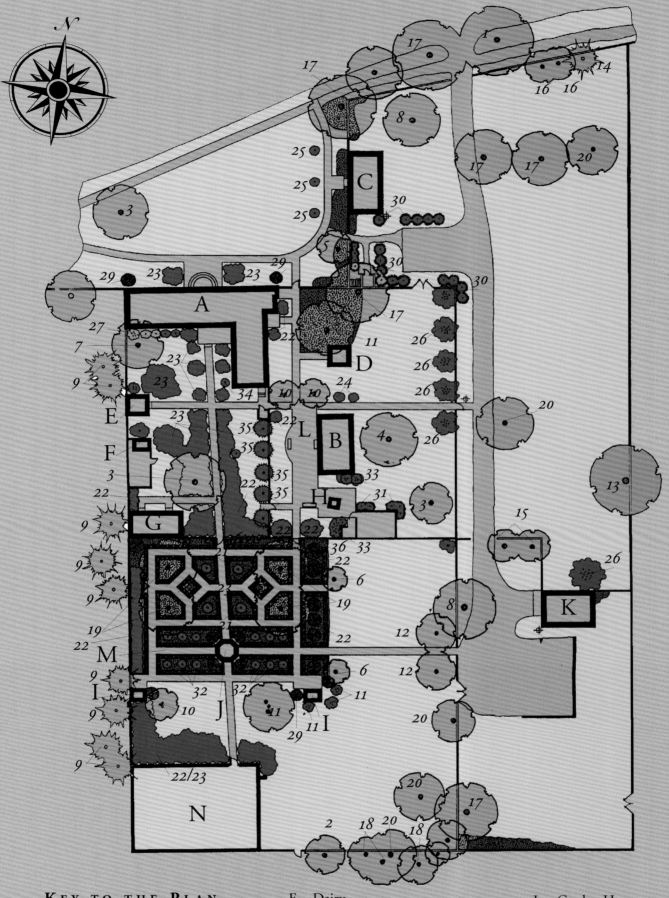

WETHERBURN'S TAVERN

ne of Williamsburg's original eighty-eight eighteenth-century buildings, Wetherburn's Tavern has been in continuous use for more than 250 years. Of Williamsburg's numerous tavern keepers, Henry Wetherburn was probably the most prosperous, at times having an interest in several taverns. Wetherburn first appeared in local records in 1731. In that year he married Mary Bowcock, a tavern keeper's widow who operated the Raleigh Tavern. When Wetherburn was granted a license to keep a tavern in August of that year, he presumably took over that operation. He was manager at the Raleigh Tavern until the early 1740s, when he moved his business across the street to the present site of Wetherburn's Tavern.

When the first Mrs. Wetherburn died in the summer of 1751, Wetherburn wasted little time in mourning, for he remarried the following week. His second wife, Anne Marot Shields, was the widow of one tavern keeper and the daughter of another. Wetherburn operated this tavern until his death in 1760.

THE WETHERBURN'S TAVERN GARDEN
The gardens at Wetherburn's have been developed to be reminiscent of the bustling, prosaic surroundings of a working tavern. To that end, reconstruction of the property has centered around the large service yard

A weathered picket fence provides the backdrop
for the kitchen garden, which contains spearmint, cabbages,
and horseradishes.

behind the tavern, an area sure to have been constantly in use during Wetherburn's time. Archaeology revealed the intricate pattern of brick, marl, and brickbats between the tavern and the kitchen.

Behind the kitchen and adjacent outbuildings is a simple square kitchen garden with a central path. It features vegetables, salad greens, and berries. Small orchards planted with plums (*Prunus domestica*), peaches (*Prunus Persica*) and sour cherries (*Prunus Cerasus*) flank the vegetable garden. A stable and small pasture complete the scene.

The contents of a well on the site examined during archaeological investigations were found to include the stones, seeds, and other remains of several common fruits and vegetables: plums, apricots, peach-es, gourds, and squash. Also discovered were twigs, needles, and branches from several trees including scrub pines, red maples, mulberries, red oaks, red cedars, black walnuts, and cottonwoods. Although this evidence is not proof that these trees were growing on the site, many have been used in the re-created garden. Major trees on the site include American elms (*Ulmus americana*), Spanish red oaks (*Quercus falcata*), red maples (*Acer rubrum*), sugar maples (*Acer saccharum*), pecans (*Carya illinoinensis*), and American lindens (*Tilia americana*).

(Above) An overview of the tavern, outbuildings, and kitchen garden at Wetherburn's. (Right) Two views of the kitchen garden.

Head cabbage.

Common onions.

KEY TO THE PLAN

A. Wetherburn's Tavern
B. Tarpley's Store
C. Kitchen
D. Dairy
E. Smokehouse
F. Well
G. Privies
H. Chicken House
I. Sheep Shelter
J. Stable
K. Kitchen Yard
L. Vegetable Garden
M. Orchard
N. Sheep Pasture

PLANT LIST

TREES

1.	Acer rubrum	Red maple
2.	Acer saccharum	Sugar maple
3.	Broussonetia papyrifera	Paper mulberry
4.	Carya illinoinensis	Pecan
5.	Cercis canadensis	Redbud
6.	Maclura pomifera	Osage orange
7.	Persea Borbonia	Red bay
8.	Prunus Cerasus	Sour cherry
9.	Prunus domestica	Common plum
10.	Prunus Persica	Peach
11.	Quercus falcata	Spanish red oak
12.	Robinia Pseudoacacia	Black locust
13.	Tilia americana	American linden
14.	Ulmus americana	American elm

SHRUBS

15.	Buxus sempervirens	Common boxwood
16.	Calycanthus floridus	Carolina allspice
17.	Ficus carica	Common fig
18.	Ilex vomitoria	Yaupon holly
19.	Myrica cerifera	Wax myrtle

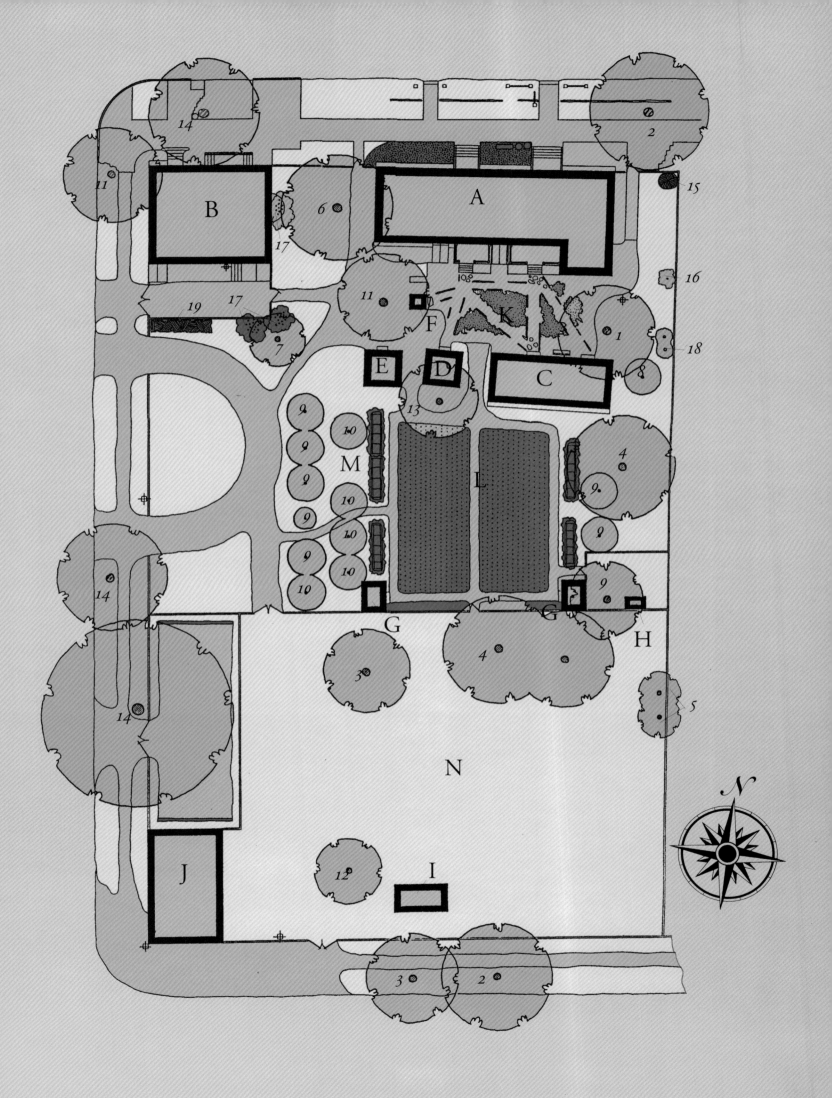

eorge Wythe married Colonel Richard Taliaferro's daughter Elizabeth about 1755. Taliaferro gave this handsome brick house on Palace green to the couple as a wedding present. Wythe was to live in the house for the next thirty-six years. In 1779, Wythe was appointed the first professor of law at the College of William and Mary. Previously, Thomas Jefferson, Henry Clay, John Marshall, and others had privately read law under Wythe's tutelage. He became one of the most influential and respected public servants of his day, first among the Virginia delegation to sign the Declaration of Independence. Wythe continued to live here after the death of his wife in 1787, but moved to Richmond in 1791. After he left Williamsburg, the property reverted to the Taliaferro estate and was put up for auction.

There was no conclusive evidence for the arrangement of the present garden and site. Insurance policies were helpful in locating the reconstructed outbuildings. Also of value to early reconstruction efforts was the survival of a copy of an early site plan of the property. The

map was drawn sometime between 1837 and 1848 by Kate Millington Blankenship, daughter of the home's owner, John Millington. The drawing showed the location of walks, outbuildings, trees, shrubs, and vegetable planting beds as they existed at the time. However accurate the drawing might have been, there was no way to determine how much or how little the site might

George Wythe by Henry Benbridge. Courtesy, R.W. Norton Art Gallery, Shreveport, La.

Native American wisteria fronts the pleasure garden at the Wythe House.

have changed in the fifty-year period between the Wythe and Millington occupancies. Other than the discovery of brickbat rubble that had been the walks behind the house, there is little archaeological evidence that indicates the garden's arrangement. Surviving letters reveal that Wythe was interested in fruit culture, but his wife apparently was in charge of the kitchen garden.

In 1770, Wythe sent Thomas Jefferson pomegranates (*Punica Granatum*) and nectarines (*Prunus Persica var. nucipersica*) from his garden, and apricot grafts and grapevines as well. Mrs. Wythe sent along some garden peas. In his journals, Jefferson also provided clues about Wythe's love of figs and his "Taliaferro Apples" named after his father-in-law, Richard Taliaferro, who had discovered them growing wild near Williamsburg.

THE GEORGE WYTHE GARDEN

The garden was designed by landscape architect Arthur A. Shurcliff and constructed in 1939–1940. Contrary to the evidence of a simple vegetable garden indicated by Kate Millington Blankenship's plan, the reconstructed gardens feature an elaborate ornamen-

(Left) The Wythe dependencies. (Above top) The pleached arbor frames the west facade of the Wythe House. (Above bottom) The dovecote in the stable yard. (Overleaf) A common plum blooms in the orchard.

The bright pink Virginia rose is another native of Virginia.

tal garden directly behind the house. In Shurcliff's original scheme, this formal garden flanked by pollarded eastern sycamores (*Platanus occidentalis*) extended west through three colonial lots terminated by a pleached American hornbeam (*Carpinus caroliniana*) arbor. Ongoing study of the properties held by Wythe led to the conclusion that the back lot had probably been used as a pasture. Therefore the stable, henhouse, and privies were relocated in 1960. The pleached hornbeam arbor also had to be moved east to the end of the central walkway where it is now located.

The topiaries and the hedging enclosing this garden were first planted in Canada hemlocks (*Tsuga canadensis*), which proved to be unreliable and were replaced with more dependable common boxwoods (*Buxus sempervirens*). The long perennial beds in this garden feature windflowers (*Anemone coronaria*) and daffodils (*Narcissus Pseudonarcissus*) for the early spring and a variety of flowering annuals for summer color. A native perennial, Stokes' asters (*Stokesia laevis*) with true blue, daisy-like flowers, are seen in the borders during the late summer months. The brick walks in this garden are based on those revealed by archaeological excavations.

Beside the churchyard brick wall are several square garden plots for vegetables and herbs. A small orchard of plums (*Prunus domestica*), black cherries (*Prunus serotina*), pears (*Pyrus communis*), and pawpaws (*Asimina triloba*) is nearby. The service yards and their various outbuildings are located to the north of the house, paralleling Prince George Street.

GEORGE WYTHE HOUSE

PLANT LIST

TREES

1.	Acer Negundo	Box elder
2.	Asimina triloba	Pawpaw
3.	Broussonetia papyrifera	Paper mulberry
4.	Carpinus caroliniana	American hornbeam
5.	Lagerstroemia indica	Crape myrtle
6.	Maclura pomifera	Osage orange
7.	Platanus occidentalis	Eastern sycamore
8.	Prunus domestica	Common plum
9.	Prunus serotina	Black cherry
10.	Pyrus communis	Common pear
11.	Quercus alba	White oak
12.	Quercus falcata	Spanish red oak
13.	Quercus virginiana	Southern live oak
14.	Robinia Pseudoacacia	Black locust
15.	Sassafras albidum	Sassafras

SHRUBS

16.	Buxus sempervirens	Common boxwood
17.	Buxus sempervirens 'Suffruticosa'	Edging boxwood
18.	Cornus Amomum	Silky dogwood
19.	Cornus racemosa	Panicled dogwood
20.	Ficus carica	Common fig
21.	Ilex vomitoria	Yaupon holly
22.	Philadelphus coronarius	Mock orange
23.	Punica Granatum	Pomegranate
24.	Rosa virginiana	Virginia rose
25.	Syringa persica	Persian lilac

VINES

26.	Campsis radicans	Trumpet creeper
27.	Lycium halimifolium	Common matrimony vine
28.	Wisteria frutescens	American wisteria

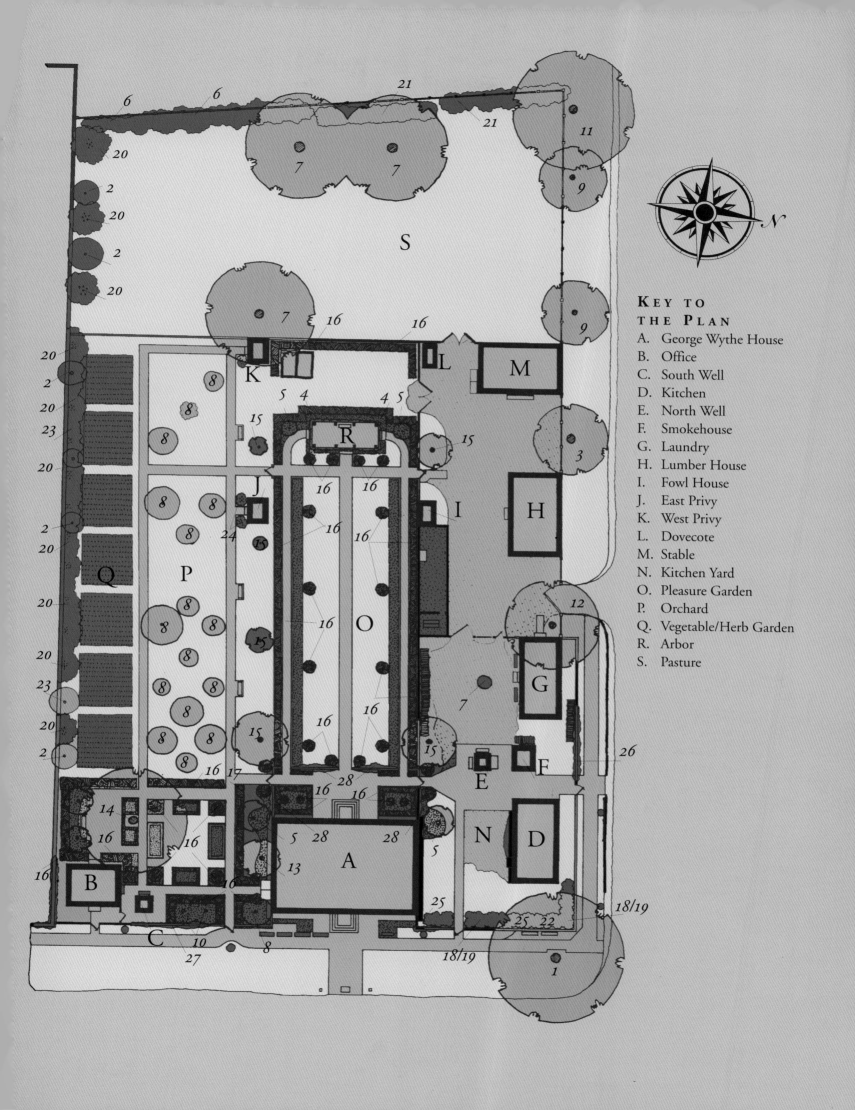

KEY TO THE PLAN

A. George Wythe House
B. Office
C. South Well
D. Kitchen
E. North Well
F. Smokehouse
G. Laundry
H. Lumber House
I. Fowl House
J. East Privy
K. West Privy
L. Dovecote
M. Stable
N. Kitchen Yard
O. Pleasure Garden
P. Orchard
Q. Vegetable/Herb Garden
R. Arbor
S. Pasture

RELATIVE FLOWERING DATES
IN THE GARDENS OF COLONIAL WILLIAMSBURG

SHRUBS	BERRIES	TREES	FLOWERS
January			
Camellia	Gold-dust tree		
Wintersweet	Beautyberry		
Witch hazel	Holly		
February			
Camellia			
Quince			
Witch hazel			
March			
Almond		Buckeye	Crocus
Pussy willow		Catalpa	Wildflowers
		Cherry	
		Pear	
		Redbud	
		Cornelian cherry	
April			
Native azaleas		Dogwood	Wildflowers
Mock orange		Mimosa	Violet
Swamp rose		Shadbush	Daffodil
Virginia rose		Silky camellia	Tulip
Scotch broom		Old-man's-beard	
Sweet shrub		Crab apple	
Mountain laurel			
Tree peony			
Lilac			
May			
Oakleaf hydrangea		Golden-rain tree	Peony
Rhododendron		Sourwood	Iris
		Tulip poplar	Old roses
		Cucumber tree	Daylily
June			
Bottlebrush Buckeye		Southern magnolia	Annuals
Fire thorn		Catalpa	Meadow wildflowers
Devil's-walking stick			
July			
Crape myrtle			
August			
		Chaste tree	Phlox
September			
			Aster
October			
	Scarlet fire thorn		
November			
Witch hazel			
Camellia			
December			
	Beautyberry		
	Dogwood		
	Washington thorn		

ANNUAL FLOWERS

Adonis aestivalis	Pheasant's-eye
Agrostemma Githago	Corn cockle
Amaranthus caudatus	Love-lies-bleeding
Amaranthus tricolor	Joseph's-coat
Anagallis arvensis	Scarlet pimpernel
Antirrhinum majus	Common snapdragon
Argemone mexicana	Mexican poppy
Aurinia saxatilis	Goldentuft
Bellis perennis	English daisy
Browallia americana	Bush violet
Calendula officinalis	Pot marigold
Callistephus chinensis	China aster
Campanula Medium	Canterbury-bells
Celosia cristata	Cockscomb
Centaurea Cineraria	Dusty-miller
Centaurea Cyanus	Cornflower
Centaurea moschata	Sweet-sultan
Cerinthe major	Honeywort
Commelina diffusa	Dayflower
Consolida ambigua	Rocket larkspur
Convolvulus tricolor	Dwarf morning-glory
Dianthus chinensis	Rainbow pink
Doronicum plantagineum	Leopard's-bane
Glaucium flavum	Horned poppy
Gomphrena globosa	Globe amaranth
Helianthus annuus	Common sunflower
Helichrysum bracteatum	Strawflower
Iberis umbellata	Globe candytuft
Impatiens Balsamina	Garden balsam
Kochia scoparia	Summer cypress
Lathyrus odoratus	Sweet pea
Lavatera trimestris	Tree mallow
Limonium sinuatum	Sea lavender
Lobelia Erinus	Edging lobelia
Lobularia maritima	Sweet alyssum
Matthiola incana	Stock
Mirabilis Jalapa	Four-o'clock
Moluccella laevis	Bells-of-Ireland
Myosotis sylvatica	Garden forget-me-not
Nicotiana alata	Flowering tobacco
Nigella damascena	Love-in-a-mist
Nolana humifusa	Nolana
Omphalodes linifolia	Navelseed
Papaver Rhoeas	Corn poppy
Papaver somniferum	Opium poppy
Pelargonium crispum	Lemon geranium
Pelargonium X domesticum	Lady Washington geranium
Reseda alba	White upright mignonette
Reseda odorata	Common mignonette
Rudbeckia hirta	Black-eyed Susan
Scabiosa atropurpurea	Sweet scabious
Tagetes erecta	African marigold
Tagetes patula	French marigold
Tropaeolum majus	Garden nasturtium
Tropaeolum minus	Dwarf nasturtium
Viola cornuta	Horned violet
Zinnia peruviana	Zinnia

ANNUAL HERBS

Anethum graveolens	Dill
Anthriscus Cerefolium	Chervil
Atriplex hortensis	Garden orach
Borago officinalis	Talewort
Carthamus tinctorius	False saffron
Coriandrum sativum	Coriander
Foeniculum vulgare	Fennel
Foeniculum vulgare azoricum	Florence fennel
Ocimum Basilicum	Sweet basil
Origanum Majorana	Sweet marjoram

Pimpinella Anisum	Common anise
Ricinus communis	Castor bean
Satureja hortensis	Summer savory
Tanacetum vulgare	Common tansy
Trigonella Foenum-graecum	Fenugreek

BULBS

Allium Ampeloprasum	Wild leek
Allium Cepa	Onion
Allium sativum	Garlic
Allium Schoenoprasum	Chive
Anemone coronaria	Windflower
Camassia scilloides	Wild hyacinth

Colchicum autumnale	Autumn crocus
Convallaria majalis	Lily-of-the-valley
Crocus sativus	Saffron crocus
Crocus vernus	Dutch crocus
Endymion hispanicus	Spanish bluebell
Endymion non-scriptus	English bluebell
Fritillaria imperialis	Crown-imperial
Fritillaria Meleagris	Checkered lily
Galanthus nivalis	Common snowdrop
Galtonia candicans	Summer hyacinth
Hyacinthus orientalis	Hyacinth
Iris reticulata	Netted iris
Iris xiphioides	English iris
Lilium canadense	Canada lily
Lilium candidum	Madonna lily
Lilium superbum	Turk's-cap lily
Muscari botryoides	Common grape hyacinth
Muscari comosum	Tassel hyacinth
Narcissus Jonquilla	Jonquil
Narcissus X odorus	Campernelle jonquil
Narcissus poeticus	Poet's narcissus
Narcissus Pseudonarcissus	Daffodil
Ornithogalum nutans	Nodding star-of-Bethlehem
Ornithogalum umbellatum	Star-of-Bethlehem
Polianthes tuberosa	Tuberose
Scilla siberica	Siberian squill
Sternbergia lutea	Winter daffodil
Tulipa chrysantha	Golden tulip
Tulipa Clusiana	Lady tulip
Tulipa Gesnerana	Tulip
Zephyranthes Atamasco	Atamasco lily

BIENNIAL FLOWERS

Alcea rosea	Hollyhock
Angelica Archangelica	Angelica
Campanula Trachelium	Nettle-leaved bellflower
Cheiranthus Cheiri	English wallflower
Dianthus barbatus	Sweet William
Digitalis purpurea	Common foxglove
Hesperis matronalis	Dame's rocket
Lunaria annua	Honesty
Oenothera biennis	Evening primrose
Viola tricolor	Johnny-jump-up

BIENNIAL HERBS

Carum Carvi	Caraway
Petroselinum crispum	Parsley
Salvia Sclarea	Clary sage

PERENNIAL FLOWERS

Achillea Millefolium	Common yarrow
Achillea Ptarmica	Sneezewort
Acorus Calamus	Sweet flag
Ajuga reptans	Carpet bugleweed
Anthemis tinctoria	Golden marguerite
Aquilegia canadensis	Wild columbine
Armeria maritima	Common thrift
Artemisia Stellerana	Dusty-miller
Asarum canadense	Wild ginger
Ascelpias tuberosa	Butterfly weed
Asphodeline lutea	Asphodel
Aster novae-angliae	New England aster
Aster novi-belgii	New York aster
Campanula persicifolia	Willow bellflower
Campanula pyramidalis	Chimney bellflower
Cassia marilandica	Wild senna
Centranthus ruber	Red valerian
Chelone glabra	Turtlehead
Chenopodium Bonus-Henricus	Good-King-Henry
Chrysanthemum indicum	Chrysanthemum
Chrysanthemum Leucanthemum	Oxeye daisy
Chrysanthemum Parthenium	Feverfew
Coreopsis lanceolata	Tickseed
Coreopsis verticillata	Threadleaf tickseed
Dianthus Caryophyllus	Clove pink
Dianthus plumarius	Grass pink
Dictamnus albus	Gas plant
Echinops Ritro	Small globe thistle
Eupatorium perfoliatum	Common boneset
Eupatorium purpureum	Joe-Pye weed
Galax urceolata	Wandflower
Gypsophila paniculata	Baby's-breath
Helenium autumnale	Sneezeweed
Heliotropium arborescens	Heliotrope
Hemerocallis fulva	Tawny daylily
Hemerocallis Lilioasphodelus	Lemon daylily
Heuchera americana	Rock geranium
Hypericum calycinum	Creeping St.-John's-wort
Hypericum densiflorum	Dense hypericum
Iberis amara	Rocket candytuft
Iberis sempervirens	Edging candytuft
Inula Helenium	Elecampane
Iris cristata	Crested iris
Iris X germanica	Flag
Iris pallida	Orris
Iris Pseudacorus	Yellow flag
Iris sibirica	Siberian iris
Linum perenne	Perennial flax
Lobelia Cardinalis	Cardinal flower
Lobelia siphilitica	Blue cardinal flower
Lychnis chalcedonica	Maltese-cross
Lychnis Coronaria	Rose campion
Mertensia virginica	Virginia bluebells
Monarda didyma	Bee balm
Monarda fistulosa	Wild bergamot
Paeonia lactiflora	Common garden peony
Papaver orientale	Oriental poppy
Phlox divaricata	Wild sweet William
Phlox paniculata	Perennial phlox
Physalis Alkekengi	Chinese-lantern
Physostegia virginiana	Obedience
Platycodon grandiflorus	Balloon flower
Pontederia cordata	Pickerel weed
Primula veris	Cowslip
Santolina Chamaecyparissus	Lavender cotton
Santolina virens	Green lavender cotton
Saponaria officinalis	Bouncing Bet
Senecio aureus	Golden groundsel
Stokesia laevis	Stokes' aster
Thermopsis caroliniana	Carolina lupine
Tiarella cordifolia	Foamflower
Tradescantia virginiana	Common spiderwort
Valeriana officinalis	Common valerian
Veronica officinalis	Common speedwell
Veronica spicata	Spike speedwell
Viola odorata	Sweet violet

PERENNIAL HERBS

Agastache Foeniculum	Anise hyssop
Aloysia triphylla	Lemon verbena
Armoracia lapathifolia	Horseradish
Artemisia Abrotanum	Southernwood
Artemisia Absinthium	Absinthe
Artemisia Dracunculus	Tarragon
Artemisia pontica	Wormwood
Chamaemelum nobile	Chamomile
Chrysanthemum Balsamita	Costmary
Chrysanthemum coccineum	Pyrethum
Cichorium Intybus	Common chicory
Galium odoratum	Sweet woodruff
Galium verum	Yellow bedstraw
Hyssopus officinalis	Hyssop
Lavandula angustifolia subsp. angustifolia	English lavender
Levisticum officinale	Lovage
Marrubium vulgare	Common horehound
Melissa officinalis	Lemon balm
Mentha X piperita	Peppermint
Mentha Pulegium	Pennyroyal
Mentha spicata	Spearmint
Mentha suaveolens	Apple mint
Mentha suaveolens 'Variegata'	Pineapple mint
Myrrhis odorata	Sweet cicely
Nepeta Cataria	Catnip
Origanum vulgare	Marjoram
Poterium Sanguisorba	Garden burnet
Pycnanthemum pilosum	Mountain mint
Rumex scutatus	French sorrel
Ruta graveolens	Common rue
Salvia azurea	Blue sage
Sanguisorba officinalis	Great burnet
Satureja montana	Winter savory
Stachys officinalis	Betony
Tanacetum vulgare	Common tansy
Taraxacum officinale	Common dandelion
Teucrium Chamaedrys	Germander
Thymus Serpyllum	Lemon thyme
Thymus vulgaris	Common thyme

SHRUBS

Acacia Farnesiana	Sweet acacia	Osmanthus americanus	Devilwood
Aesculus parviflora	Bottlebrush buckeye	Paeonia suffruticosa	Tree peony
Aronia arbutifolia	Red chokeberry	Philadelphus coronarius	Mock orange
Aucuba japonica	Japanese aucuba	Pieris floribunda	Fetterbush
Aucuba japonica		Prunus glandulosa	Flowering almond
Variegata	Gold-dust tree	Prunus maritima	Beach plum
Baccharis halimifolia	Groundsel tree	Punica Granatum	Pomegranate
Buxus sempervirens	Common boxwood	Pyracantha coccinea	Fire thorn
Buxus sempervirens		Rhododendron	
'Arborescens'	Tree boxwood	calendulaceum	Flame azalea
Buxus sempervirens		Rhododendron	
'Suffruticosa'	Edging boxwood	periclymenoides	Pinxterbloom
Callicarpa americana	Beautyberry	Rhododendron viscosum	Swamp azalea
Calycanthus floridus	Carolina allspice	Rhus aromatica	Fragrant sumac
Camellia japonica	Common camellia	Rhus copallina	Shining sumac
Camellia sinensis	Tea plant	Rhus glabra	Smooth sumac
Caragana arborescens	Siberian pea tree	Rhus typhina	Staghorn sumac
Ceanothus americanus	New Jersey tea	Ribes nigrum	European black
Celastrus scandens	American bittersweet		currant
Cephalanthus		Robinia hispida	Rose acacia
occidentalis	Buttonbush	Rosa canina	Dog rose
Chaenomeles speciosa	Flowering quince	Rosa centifolia	Cabbage rose
Chimonanthus praecox	Wintersweet	Rosa centifolia	
Clethra alnifolia	Summer-sweet	'Muscosa'	Moss rose
Comptonia peregrina	Sweet fern	Rosa chinensis	
Cornus alba 'Sibirica'	Siberian dogwood	'Old Blush'	Old blush rose
Cornus Amomum	Silky dogwood	Rosa damascena	Damask rose
Cornus racemosa	Panicled dogwood	Rosa damascena	
Cornus sericea	Red-osier dogwood	'Versicolor'	York-and-Lancaster rose
Cyrilla racemiflora	Leatherwood	Rosa Eglanteria	Sweetbrier rose
Danae racemosa	Alexandrian laurel	Rosa gallica	French rose
Elaeagnus angustifolia	Russian olive	Rosa gallica	
Euonymus americana	Strawberry bush	'Officinalis'	Apothecary rose
Ficus carica	Common fig	Rosa gallica	
Forestiera acuminata	Swamp privet	'Versicolor'	Rosa Mundi rose
Fothergilla Gardenii	Witch alder	Rosa laevigata	Cherokee rose
Gardenia jasminoides	Common gardenia	Rosa palustris	Swamp rose
Hibiscus syriacus	Rose-of-Sharon	Rosa Roxburghii	Chestnut rose
Hydrangea arborescens	Wild hydrangea	Rosa spinosissima	Scotch rose
Hydrangea quercifolia	Oakleaf hydrangea	Rosa virginiana	Virginia rose
Ilex decidua	Possum haw	Rosmarinus officinalis	Rosemary
Ilex glabra	Inkberry	Rubus odoratus	Flowering raspberry
Ilex verticillata	Winterberry	Ruscus aculeatus	Butcher's-broom
Ilex vomitoria	Yaupon holly	Salix discolor	Pussy willow
Illicium floridanum	Purple anise tree	Salvia officinalis	Garden sage
Itea virginica	Sweetspire	Spiraea tomentosa	Hardhack
Kalmia latifolia	Mountain laurel	Staphylea trifolia	American bladdernut
Laurus nobilis	Laurel	Symphoricarpos	
Leucothoe axillaris	Coast leucothoe	orbiculatus	Indian currant
Leucothoe Fontanesiana	Drooping leucothoe	Syringa X chinensis	Chinese lilac
Lindera Benzoin	Spicebush	Syringa Josikaea	Hungarian lilac
Lonicera tatarica	Tatarian honeysuckle	Syringa X persica	Persian lilac
Myrica cerifera	Wax myrtle	Syringa vulgaris	Common lilac
Myrtus communis	Myrtle	Taxus baccata	English yew
Nerium Oleander	Common oleander	Vaccinium corymbosum	Highbush blueberry
		Vaccinum stamineum	Deerberry
		Viburnum acerifolium	Maple-leaved viburnum
		Viburnum cassinoides	Withe-rod
		Viburnum dentatum	Southern arrowwood
		Viburnum Lantana	Wayfaring tree
		Viburnum Lentago	Nannyberry
		Viburnum nudum	Smooth withe-rod
		Viburnum Opulus	Cranberry bush
		Viburnum prunifolium	Black haw
		Viburnum Tinus	Laurustinus viburnum
		Viburnum trilobum	Highbush cranberry
		Vitex Agnus-castus	Chaste tree
		Vitex Negundo	
		var. 'heterophylla'	Cutleaf chaste tree
		Yucca aloifolia	Spanish-bayonet
		Yucca filamentosa	Adam's-needle

TREES

Acer Negundo	Box elder
Acer platanoides	Norway maple
Acer rubrum	Red maple
Acer saccharinum	Silver maple
Acer saccharum	Sugar maple
Aesculus Hippocastanum	Horse chestnut
Aesculus Pavia	Red buckeye
Aesculus X plantierensis	Pink-flowering horse chestnut
Ailanthus altissima	Tree-of-heaven
Albizia Julibrissin	Mimosa
Amelanchier canadensis	Shadbush
Aralia spinosa	Devil's-walking stick
Asimina triloba	Pawpaw
Betula nigra	River birch
Broussonetia papyrifera	Paper mulberry
Bumelia lanuginosa	Chittamwood
Carpinus caroliniana	American hornbeam
Carya illinoinensis	Pecan
Catalpa bignonioides	Common catalpa
Catalpa speciosa	Western catalpa
Cedrus libani	Cedar-of-Lebanon
Celtis laevigata	Mississippi hackberry
Celtis occidentalis	Sugarberry
Cercis canadensis	Redbud
Chamaecyparis thyoides	White cedar
Chionanthus virginicus	Old-man's-beard
Cladrastis lutea	Yellowwood
Cornus florida	Flowering dogwood
Cornus florida 'Rubra'	Pink-flowering dogwood
Cornus mas	Cornelian cherry
Corylus americana	American hazelnut
Cotinus Coggygria	Smoke tree
Crataegus Phaenopyrum	Washington thorn
Cydonia oblonga	Common quince
Diospyros virginiana	Common persimmon
Eriobotrya japonica	Loquat
Fagus grandifolia	American beech
Franklinia Alatamaha	Franklin tree
Fraxinus americana	White ash
Fraxinus pennsylvanica	Green ash
Ginkgo biloba	Maidenhair tree
Gleditsia triacanthos	Honey locust
Gymnocladus dioica	Kentucky coffee tree
Halesia carolina	Wild olive
Hamamelis virginiana	Witch hazel
Ilex Aquifolium	English holly
Ilex Cassine	Dahoon holly
Ilex Cassine var. 'myrtifolia'	Myrtle-leaved holly
Ilex opaca	American holly
Juglans cinerea	Butternut
Juglans nigra	Black walnut
Juglans regia	English walnut
Juniperus virginiana	Red cedar
Koelreuteria paniculata	Golden-rain tree
Laburnum anagyroides	Golden-chain
Lagerstroemia indica	Crape myrtle
Liquidambar Styraciflua	Sweet gum
Liriodendron Tulipifera	Tulip poplar
Maclura pomifera	Osage orange
Magnolia acuminata	Cucumber tree
Magnolia grandiflora	Southern magnolia
Magnolia virginiana	Sweet bay
Malus angustifolia	Southern wild crab apple
Malus coronaria	Wild sweet crab apple
Malus pumila	Common apple
Melia Azedarach	Chinaberry
Mespilus germanica	Medlar
Morus alba	White mulberry
Morus rubra	Red mulberry
Nyssa sylvatica	Black gum
Oxydendrum arboreum	Sourwood
Persea Borbonia	Red bay
Picea Abies	Norway spruce
Pinus Strobus	Eastern white pine
Pinus Taeda	Loblolly pine
Pinus virginiana	Scrub pine
Platanus occidentalis	Eastern sycamore
Populus deltoides	Cottonwood
Populus nigra 'Italica'	Lombardy poplar
Prunus Armeniaca	Apricot
Prunus caroliniana	Cherry laurel
Prunus cerasifera	Myrobalan plum
Prunus Cerasus	Sour cherry
Prunus domestica	Common plum
Prunus Persica	Peach
Prunus Persica var. nucipersica	Nectarine
Prunus serotina	Black cherry
Ptelea trifoliata	Stinking ash
Pyrus communis	Common pear
Quercus alba	White oak
Quercus coccinea	Scarlet oak
Quercus falcata	Spanish red oak
Quercus imbricaria	Shingle oak
Quercus laurifolia	Laurel oak
Quercus marilandica	Blackjack oak
Quercus nigra	Water oak
Quercus palustris	Pin oak
Quercus phellos	Willow oak
Quercus rubra	Red oak
Quercus velutina	Black oak
Quercus virginiana	Southern live oak
Robinia Pseudoacacia	Black locust
Salix babylonica	Weeping willow
Salix nigra	Black willow
Sambucus canadensis	American elder
Sassafras albidum	Sassafras
Sorbus americana	American mountain ash
Stewartia Malacodendron	Silky camellia
Stewartia ovata	Mountain camellia
Taxodium distichum	Bald cypress
Thuja occidentalis	American arborvitae
Tilia americana	American linden
Tilia cordata	Small-leaved European linden
Tsuga canadensis	Canada hemlock
Ulmus alata	Winged elm
Ulmus americana	American elm
Ulmus procera	English elm
Ulmus rubra	Slippery elm

VINES

Bignonia capreolata	Cross vine
Campsis radicans	Trumpet creeper
Clematis virginiana	Virgin's bower
Decumaria barbara	Wood-vamp
Gelsemium sempervirens	Carolina jessamine
Hedera Helix	English ivy
Hydrangea anomala petiolaris	Climbing hydrangea
Jasminum officinale	Poet's jessamine
Lonicera sempervirens	Coral honeysuckle
Lycium halimifolium	Common matrimony vine
Parthenocissus quinquefolia	Virginia creeper
Vinca major	Greater periwinkle
Vinca minor	Common periwinkle
Vitis Labrusca	Fox grape
Vitis rotundifolia	Muscadine grape
Wisteria frutescens	American wisteria
Wisteria sinensis	Chinese wisteria

BIBLIOGRAPHY

Adams, William Howard. *Nature Perfected: Gardens Through History.* New York: Abbeville Press, 1991.

Betts, Edwin M., and Hazlehurst Bolton Perkins. *Thomas Jefferson's Flower Garden at Monticello.* 3rd ed. revised and enlarged by Peter J. Hatch. Charlottesville, Va.: University Press of Virginia, 1986.

Betts, Edwin Morris, ed. *Thomas Jefferson's Garden Book, 1766–1824.* Philadelphia: American Philosophical Society, 1944.

Carson, Jane. *We Were There: Descriptions of Williamsburg, 1699–1859.* Williamsburg, Va.: Colonial Williamsburg Foundation, 1965.

Chambers, Douglas. *The Planters of the English Landscape Garden: Botany, Trees, and the* Georgics. New Haven, Conn.: Yale University Press, 1993.

Coats, Alice M. *Flowers and their Histories.* London: Adam & Charles Black, 1968.

———. *Garden Shrubs and their Histories.* Rev. ed. New York: Simon and Schuster, 1992.

de Bray, Lys. *Lys de Bray's Manual of Old-Fashioned Flowers.* Sparkford, Yeovil, Somerset, Eng.: Oxford Illustrated Press, 1984.

de Forest, Elizabeth Kellam. *The Gardens & Grounds at Mount Vernon: How George Washington Planned and Planted Them.* Mount Vernon, Va.: Mount Vernon Ladies' Association of the Union, 1982.

Dutton, Joan Parry. *The Flower World of Williamsburg.* Rev. ed. Williamsburg, Va.: Colonial Williamsburg Foundation, 1973.

———. *Plants of Colonial Williamsburg.* Williamsburg, Va.: Colonial Williamsburg Foundation, 1979.

Favretti, Rudy J. *Gardens & Landscapes of Virginia.* Little Compton, R. I.: Fort Church Publishers, Inc., 1993.

Favretti, Rudy F., and Gordon P. DeWolf. *Colonial Gardens.* Barre, Mass.: Barre Publishers, 1972.

Favretti, Rudy J., and Joy P. Favretti. *For Every House A Garden: A guide for reproducing period gardens.* Chester, Conn.: Pequot Press, 1977.

Favretti, Rudy J., and Joy Putman Favretti. *Landscapes and Gardens for Historic Buildings: A handbook for reproducing and creating authentic landscape settings.* 2nd rev. ed. Nashville, Tenn.: American Association for State and Local History, 1991.

Frye, Harriet. *The Great Forest, John Clayton and Flora: A Narrative Biography of America's First Botanist.* Hampton, Va.: Dragon Run Books, 1990.

Gardner, Jo Ann. *The Heirloom Garden: Selecting & Growing Over 300 Old-Fashioned Ornamentals.* Pownal, Vt.: Storey Communications, Inc., 1992.

Halliwell, Brian. *Old Garden Flowers.* London: Bishopsgate Press, Ltd., 1987.

Hatch, Peter J. *The Gardens of Monticello.* Charlottesville, Va.: Thomas Jefferson Memorial Foundation, Inc., 1992.

Hedrick, U. P. *A History of Horticulture in America to 1860.* Reprint ed. Portland, Ore.: Timber Press, 1988.

Hobhouse, Penelope. *Gardening Through the Ages: An Illustrated History of Plants and Their Influence on Garden Styles—from Ancient Egypt to the Present Day.* New York: Simon and Schuster, 1992.

Hussey, Christopher. *English Gardens and Landscape, 1700–1750.* London: Country Life Limited, 1967.

Jabs, Carolyn. *The Heirloom Gardener.* San Francisco, Calif.: Sierra Club Books, 1984.

Jackson, John Brinckerhoff. *Discovering the Vernacular Landscape.* New Haven, Conn.: Yale University Press, 1984.

Jackson-Stops, Gervase. *The Country House Garden: A Grand Tour.* London: Pavilion Books, Ltd., 1987.

Jacques, David, and Arend Jan van der Horst. *The Gardens of William and Mary.* London: Christopher Helm, 1988.

Jellicoe, Geoffrey, Susan Jellicoe, Patrick Goode, and Michael Lancaster. *The Oxford Companion to Gardens.* New York: Oxford University Press, 1986.

Keen, Mary. *The Glory of the English Garden.* Boston: Little Brown and Co., Inc., 1989.

Kelly, Mary Palmer. *The Early English Kitchen Garden.* Columbia, S. C.: Garden History Associates, 1984.

Kornwolf, James D. *"So Good A Design": The Colonial Campus of the College of William and Mary: Its History, Background, and Legacy.* Williamsburg, Va.: College of William and Mary Joseph and Margaret Muscarelle Museum of Art, 1989.

Laird, Mark. *The Formal Garden: Traditions of Art and Nature.* London: Thames and Hudson, Ltd., 1992.

Leighton, Ann. *American Gardens in the Eighteenth Century: "For Use or for Delight."* Boston: Houghton Mifflin Co., 1976.

————. *Early American Gardens: "For Meate or Medicine."* Boston: Houghton Mifflin Co., 1970.

Le Rougetel, Hazel. *The Chelsea Gardener: Philip Miller, 1691–1771.* Portland, Ore.: Sagapress, Inc./Timber Press, Inc., in association with Natural History Publications, London, 1990.

Llewellyn, Roddy. *Ornamental English Gardens.* New York: Rizzoli, 1990.

Lounsbury, Carl, ed. *An Illustrated Glossary of Early Southern Architecture and Landscape.* New York: Oxford University Press, 1994.

Lowenthal, David, and Marcus Binney, eds. *Our Past Before Us: Why Do We Save It?* London: Temple Smith, Ltd., 1981.

Maccubbin, Robert P., and Peter Martin. *British and American Gardens in the Eighteenth Century.* Williamsburg, Va.: Colonial Williamsburg Foundation, 1984.

Martin, Laura C. *Garden Flower Folklore.* Chester, Conn.: Globe Pequot Press, 1987.

Martin, Peter. *The Pleasure Gardens of Virginia: From Jamestown to Jefferson.* Princeton, N. J.: Princeton University Press, 1991.

Mathes, Martin C. *The Planting of a Campus Tradition: A History of the Landscape of the College of William and Mary.* Rev. ed. Williamsburg, Va.: College of William and Mary, 1992.

Noël Hume, Audrey. *Archaeology and the Colonial Gardener.* Williamsburg, Va.: Colonial Williamsburg Foundation, 1974.

Pregill, Phillip, and Nancy Volkman. *Landscapes in History: Design and Planning in the Western Tradition.* New York: Van Nostrand Reinhold, 1993.

Proctor Rob. *Antique Flowers: Annuals: Yearly Classics for the Contemporary Garden.* New York: Harper Collins, 1991.

————. *Antique Flowers: Perennials: Enduring Classics for the Contemporary Garden.* New York: Harper & Row, 1990.

Punch, Walter T., ed. *Keeping Eden: A History of Gardening in America.* Boston: Little Brown and Co., Inc., for the Massachusetts Horticultural Society, 1992.

Reps, John W. *Tidewater Towns: City Planning in Colonial Virginia and Maryland.* Williamsburg, Va.: Colonial Williamsburg Foundation, 1972.

Robinson, William. *The English Flower Garden.* New York: Amaryllis Press, 1984.

Rose, Graham. *The Classic Garden.* New York: Summit Books, 1989.

Scott-James, Anne, and Osbert Lancaster. *The Pleasure Garden: An Illustrated History of British Gardening.* London: John Murray, 1977.

Stilgoe, John R. *Common Landscape of America, 1580 to 1845.* New Haven, Conn.: Yale University Press, 1982.

Strong, Roy. *The Renaissance Garden in England.* London: Thames and Hudson, Ltd., 1979.

Stuart, David, and James Sutherland. *Plants from the Past.* New York: Viking, 1987.

Taylor, Patrick. *Period Gardens: New Life for Historic Landscapes.* New York: Atlantic Monthly Press, 1991.

Thomas, Graham Stuart, ed. *Recreating the Period Garden.* Boston: David R. Godine, 1985.

Triggs, H. Inigo. *Formal Gardens in England and Scotland.* 2nd ed. Woodbridge, Suffolk, Eng.: Antique Collectors' Club, 1988.

Turner, Tom. *English Garden Design: History and styles since 1650.* Woodbridge, Suffolk, Eng.: Antique Collectors' Club, 1986.

Whiteside, Katherine. *Antique Flowers: A Guide to Using Old-Fashioned Species in Contemporary Gardens.* New York: Villard Books, 1989.

Williams, Dorothy Hunt. *Historic Virginia Gardens: Preservations of the Garden Club of Virginia.* Charlottesville, Va.: University Press of Virginia, 1975.

Williamsburg's Joseph Prentis: His Monthly Kalender & Garden Book. Chillicothe, Ill.: American Botanist, Booksellers, 1992.

Wright, Richardson. *The Story of Gardening: From the Hanging Gardens of Babylon to the Hanging Gardens of New York.* New York: Dodd, Mead & Co., 1934.

INDEX